# Transforming *the* Development Landscape

# Transforming *the* Development Landscape

## The Role of the Private Sector

LAEL BRAINARD, *editor*

BROOKINGS INSTITUTION PRESS
*Washington, D.C.*

1775 Massachusetts Avenue, N.W., Washington, D.C. 20036
www.brookings.edu



*Library of Congress Cataloging-in-Publication data*
Transforming the development landscape : the role of the private sector / Lael Brainard, editor.
p. cm.
Includes bibliographical references and index.
ISBN-13: 978-0-8157-1124-7 (pbk. : alk. paper)
ISBN-10: 0-8157-1124-7 (pbk. : alk. paper)
1. Economic development projects—Developing countries—Finance. 2. Private enterprise—Developing countries. 3. Business enterprises —Developing countries. 4. Investments, Foreign—Developing countries. I. Brainard, Lael.
HC59.72.E44T72 2006
338.9009172′4—dc22 2006021492

9 8 7 6 5 4 3 2 1

The paper used in this publication meets minimum requirements of the American National Standard for Information Sciences—Permanence of Paper for Printed Library Materials: ANSI Z39.48-1992.

Typeset in Adobe Garamond

Composition by Cynthia Stock
Silver Spring, Maryland

Printed by Victor Graphics
Baltimore, Maryland

# *Contents*

# *Foreword*

THE NEW MILLENNIUM has ushered in a heightened public awareness of global poverty and a renewed spirit of generosity among developed nations. So far, the public agenda has focused primarily on boosting official assistance and canceling official debt, with much less attention directed at the most dynamic engine of growth and poverty alleviation: the private sector. Yet private enterprise belongs at the very center of the development enterprise. By generating jobs, serving the underserved, promoting innovation, and spurring productivity, indigenous private sector development can raise living standards and promote opportunity. Indeed, leaders of poor nations have placed private sector development high on their own priority list. *Transforming the Development Landscape: The Role of the Private Sector* provides in-depth analysis of the role of the private sector in development.

This volume, edited by Lael Brainard, includes chapters by Warrick Smith of the World Bank, Jane Nelson of Harvard University, Timothy Freundlich of the Calvert Social Investment Foundation, Ross Levine of Brown University, Alan Patricof of Apax Partners, Julie Sunderland, David de Ferranti of the Brookings Institution, Larry Cooley of Management Systems International, and Rajiv Shah and Sylvia Mathews of the Gates Foundation. The chapters draw from a conference at the Aspen Institute from August 3 to August 6, 2005, when fifty preeminent international leaders from the public, private, and nonprofit sectors came together to address "The Private Sector's Role in the Fight against Global Poverty." The conference was hosted by

Richard C. Blum of Blum Capital Partners and Lael Brainard and myself of the Brookings Institution, with the active support of honorary cochairs Walter Isaacson of the Aspen Institute and Mary Robinson of Realizing Rights: The Ethical Globalization Initiative.

Special thanks are due to Zoe Konovalov for her excellent contribution as the project director for this volume and to Raji Jagadeesan, Emily McWithey, Nicholas Warren, and Molly Langer for superb research and planning support.

The editor wishes to thank Alfred Imhoff for outstanding and rapid editing, Inge Lockwood for copy editing, Andrew Mast and Tristan Reed for help with the web version of the report, and Janet Walker and Susan Woollen of the Brookings Institution Press. The authors remain responsible for their chapters and their content and any errors or omissions.

This book was made possible by generous support from Richard C. Blum, chairman of Blum Capital Partners, and the Ewing Marion Kauffman Foundation.

Strobe Talbott
*President*

*Washington, D.C.*
*June 2006*

# Transforming *the* Development Landscape

# 1

## *The Private Sector in the Fight against Global Poverty*

LAEL BRAINARD AND VINCA LAFLEUR

A TRIO OF KEY INTERNATIONAL meetings marked 2005 as a pivotal year for the global antipoverty movement: the Gleneagles Group of Eight (G-8) Summit in July, where British prime minister Tony Blair pledged to put Africa's challenges front and center; the United Nations General Assembly's review of the Millennium Development Goals in September; and the World Trade Organization's ministerial meeting in December, where the fate of the Doha Development Agenda hung in the balance. Each meeting offered opportunities to help turn the tide on global poverty.

At the same time, civil society groups were mobilizing worldwide to prod political leaders toward action. From the ONE Campaign in the United States to the United Kingdom's "Make Poverty History" movement, broad-based

**Lael Brainard** is the vice president and director of the Global Economy and Development Program and holds the Bernard L. Schwartz Chair in International Economics at the Brookings Institution. She served as the deputy assistant to the president for international economic policy and U.S. sherpa to the G-8 in the Clinton administration and as an associate professor of applied economics at the Massachusetts Institute of Technology Sloan School. She received master's and doctoral degrees in economics from Harvard University, where she was a National Science Foundation Fellow.

**Vinca LaFleur** is a visiting fellow at the Center for Strategic and International Studies and president of a communications practice in Washington, D.C. Previously, she served on the National Security Council staff as a speechwriter and special assistant to President Bill Clinton. She is a graduate of Yale University and the Johns Hopkins School of Advanced International Studies.

The authors wish to thank Zoe Konovalov, Raji Jagadeesan, and Nicholas Warren for their invaluable insights and superb assistance in writing this chapter.

coalitions were pressuring national governments for vastly increased aid, fair trade, and debt cancellation.

Meanwhile, prominent public figures added celebrity appeal to the cause. Rock star Bono's tireless work against poverty earned him a Nobel Peace Prize nomination; Bob Geldof staged six "Live 8" rock-stravaganzas in advance of the G-8 summit; in Trafalgar Square, Nelson Mandela urged young people to wear a white armband to demonstrate their commitment to combating poverty; and Bill Clinton hosted the high-profile Clinton Global Initiative in New York, which focused in large part on the escape from poverty.

The media also trained their powerful spotlight on the world's poorest people—from *Time* magazine devoting a cover story to global poverty to MTV broadcasting *The Diary of Angelina Jolie and Dr. Jeffrey Sachs in Africa.* And a string of natural disasters—the South Asian tsunami, the Niger drought, Hurricane Katrina, and the earthquake in Pakistan and Kashmir—reminded the world's people of our common humanity and galvanized an outpouring of assistance.

This heightened public awareness of global poverty and renewed spirit of generosity are welcome advances in the work of development. So far, however, the public agenda has focused primarily on boosting official assistance and canceling official debt. Even though the past two decades have witnessed an enormous shift in resources away from the public sector to private hands, and private flows to developing countries are now more than twice the level of public flows, scant attention has been directed at the most dynamic engine of growth and poverty alleviation: the private sector. Indeed, the private sector merits only two very narrow mentions in the Millennium Development Goals.[1]

Yet private enterprise belongs at the very center of the development enterprise. By generating jobs, serving the underserved, promoting innovation, and spurring productivity, indigenous private sector development can raise living standards and promote opportunity (Klein and Hadjimichael 2003; Porter 2004; United Nations Commission on the Private Sector and Development 2004). The most dramatic example is China, whose surging growth has raised 400 million people from poverty in the past two decades.

Moreover, rich and poor consumers alike benefit from the lower prices

1. In targets 17 and 18, respectively, donor governments are directed to work in partnership with pharmaceutical companies in providing essential medicines and with the private sector in making available the benefits of new technologies. See United Nations Millennium Development Goals (www.un.org/millenniumgoals/).

and greater choices that competition brings. Private firms are also the main source of tax revenues for social services like health care and education. And given the right circumstances, the entrepreneurial spirit can be sparked within any society—bringing a spirit of internal empowerment. No wonder, then, that leaders of poor nations have placed private sector development high on their own priority lists—as shown, for instance, by the homegrown New Partnership for African Development and more recently in the Commission for Africa report.[2]

But just as an indigenous private sector can be a powerful force for change, so too does the global private sector have a positive role to play in development. As the Harvard University scholar Jane Nelson notes, business leaders can make a difference through "the implementation of responsible business practices and standards, in areas such as ethics, the environment, labor, and human rights, . . . [by] harnessing the core competencies, resources, and problem-solving skills of private enterprise to create new social and market value; and . . . [by] working in partnership with others to help establish the appropriate enabling environment or conditions for good governance and private sector development."[3] Whether by paying premium prices for coffee produced with sustainable practices, donating resources to build schools and hospitals, or championing improved market access for developing country exports, a multinational firm can bring unique resources, leverage, and experience to the development table.

Moreover, the private sector can bring to the fight against global poverty the same spirit of leadership, innovation, and initiative—and the same skills in scaling size up, driving costs down, and reaching out to new clients—that success in the global marketplace requires. And in contrast to the slow and uncertain pace of the public sector in making budget appropriations or adopting reforms, the private sector has the power to take meaningful steps against poverty right away.

For the world's neediest people, such a commitment by the private sector cannot come soon enough. Children are starving in an age of abundance, ailing in an era of medical miracles, and perishing in extreme poverty at a rate of 1,200 each hour. The ways and means exist to save these children, if the world can find the will.

2. Commission for Africa, *Our Common Interest, Report of the Commission for Africa,* 2005 (www.commissionforafrica.org/english/report/introduction.html).

3. See Jane Nelson, "Leveraging the Development Impact of Business in the Fight against Global Poverty," chapter 3 in this volume.

## Empowering Business to Do Business in the Developing World

The dynamic growth of the private sector in poor countries is indispensable if the international community is to meet its pledge in the Millennium Development Goals to halve extreme poverty by 2015. As UN secretary general Kofi Annan has said, "We cannot reach these goals without the support of the private sector. Most of all, we cannot reach them without a strong private sector in the developing countries themselves, to create jobs and bring prosperity."

Indeed, because top-down approaches to development have failed to produce consistent results, appreciation for the role of private enterprise in generating durable growth is increasing. International agencies like the United Nations Development Program are assigning a higher priority to the issue; the program's influential Commission on the Private Sector and Development produced a report titled "Unleashing Entrepreneurship," which the G-8 leaders endorsed at their 2004 summit (UN Commission on the Private Sector and Development). Meanwhile, the World Bank is strengthening its traditional commitment to private sector development; its *World Development Report 2005* drew on surveys of nearly 30,000 firms in fifty-three developing countries to explain and measure the forces shaping their investment climates.

At the same time, civil society groups are showing a greater interest in working with private partners on poverty reduction and vice versa. Gone are the days when nongovernmental organizations (NGOs) demonized big business as the enemy and corporations caricatured activists as tree-hugging idealists. After all, private enterprise is the greatest source of self-employment and jobs—the two factors poor people themselves rank highest as means to improve their own lives. Together, business and civil society are devising creative alliances to advance shared development goals in areas such as microfinance and resource transparency.

Yet despite a growing recognition of the importance of entrepreneurship in defeating poverty and spurring growth, private enterprise still is not thriving uniformly across the developing world. Why does it flourish in some societies while suffocating in others? What can be done to unleash entrepreneurship's contribution to development?

Among the many avenues to explore are three fundamental questions: How can the climate be improved for private enterprise in developing countries? Do certain sizes or types of enterprises contribute more powerfully than others to productivity growth, innovation, and employment? And how can more private capital investment be channeled to poor countries?

### Improving the Climate for Private Enterprise

In the words of Warrick Smith of the World Bank Group's Vice Presidency for Private Sector Development, "Firms and entrepreneurs invest and make productivity improvements not out of any sense of philanthropy but to make profits. Their decisions are thus influenced by the expected risks and rewards associated with alternative courses of action. Those risks and rewards are in turn shaped by the investment climate. . . . But what shapes the investment climate?"[4]

Some of the factors shaping the climate for private enterprise are difficult to change. A geographically remote or rugged country will inherently face transportation challenges, just as a small or sparsely populated country will have a limited market size. Social attitudes toward risk and failure can constitute serious barriers to entrepreneurial growth; in some poor countries, creativity and innovation are not adequately rewarded or valued. Cultural barriers and norms may disproportionately impede certain groups such as women and minorities.

But research shows that government policies and behaviors have a critical role to play (World Bank 2004a, 2004b, 2005, 2006). If governments can put the right market-friendly framework in place, the private sector's ability to spark growth and alleviate poverty can be markedly improved.

Several policy and regulatory levers can prove especially significant: ensuring effective financial intermediation; assigning property rights—including those of poor people, as Hernando de Soto has persuasively argued; enforcing contracts; and fostering predictable policies and a sound macroeconomic environment. In fact, World Bank research shows that "improving policy certainty alone could increase the likelihood of new investment by over 30 percent."[5] Where the rule of law is weak, transactions must rely on personal relationships, greatly undermining the efficiency of financial intermediation and reducing productive investment.

Regulations facilitating firm entry and exit—along with relatively open trade policies—can contribute to a greater degree of competition, lower prices, and more consumer choices. World Bank research shows that the

4. See Warrick Smith, "Unleashing Entrepreneurship," chapter 2 in this volume.
5. See Warrick Smith, "Unleashing Entrepreneurship," chapter 2 in this volume.

number of days required to open a business tends to be significantly higher in low-income countries; it ranges from two in Australia to 203 in Haiti. In an unprecedented move, the U.S. Millennium Challenge Corporation has adopted this competitiveness indicator as a criterion for eligibility. But other procedures can exact a huge toll on the private sector in poor countries as well; for example, enforcing a simple contract takes 1,459 days in Guatemala, according to the World Bank, as compared with only forty-eight in the Netherlands.[6]

Of course, while identifying key drivers and constraints to private investment is relatively straightforward, actually making lasting policy reforms is not. For one thing, those who benefit from the status quo may have significant political clout to resist change, and incentives may not be sufficient or appropriately aligned to achieve results. In addition, conditions for private enterprise may vary not only among countries but within them, as different sectors or different classes of enterprise face different hurdles. And complex unknowns surround the sequencing of reform efforts and the interaction of different policy and regulatory changes. Setting priorities is difficult when so much is crying out to be done.

Although the necessary political will must come from within developing countries themselves, the international community does have some useful points of leverage—such as supporting the development of pro-reform political forces, small business associations, and influential diaspora communities, all of which can create demand-side pressure for otherwise unpopular reforms. And trade agreements can help developing country governments lock in a reform agenda, reinforcing investor confidence that reforms will be sustained.

Similarly, though legitimate debates persist over how to prioritize reforms, the challenges of sequencing should not become a smoke screen for complacency. Creating a good climate for private enterprise is a long-term process. The full set of necessary reforms cannot and need not be attained simultaneously. What counts is sustained progress.

A corollary is that adopting appropriate laws and policies is necessary—but will not be enough on its own. Often, deeper challenges inhibit private sector growth—such as a lack of policy credibility and poor public trust. Corruption is a particularly corrosive force that undermines vibrant private sectors and helps to perpetuate poverty. In the words of the Tanzanian entrepreneur Ali Mufuruki, "The biggest problem in Africa today is not poverty

6. World Bank, Country Data Profile, http://doingbusiness.org/Documents/2006-country-tables.pdf.

caused by historical conditions but by people themselves. We have good examples of countries built and wrecked again by their own people. People need to take responsibility to make their governments deliver."

And, of course, private enterprise depends as well on important enabling factors, ranging from a skilled work force and adequate infrastructure to contact with potential customers, connections to suppliers, access to know-how and technology, and, crucially, access to capital—a problem that is especially acute with regard to seed funding for early-stage enterprises and risk capital for expansion.

Liberating entrepreneurship in developing countries is not as simple as "if we build a business-friendly policy environment, they will come." Instead, it involves meeting the manifold challenges sketched in this chapter, which in turn requires commitment and creativity from a range of stakeholders. It also requires a clear understanding of ultimate goals and objectives, as there may be a trade-off between those measures that will help the very poorest citizens of a country and those that will spark the long-term growth of its whole economy.

But most immediately, unleashing entrepreneurship requires the courage to act—recognizing that while a vigorous private sector is not enough by itself to end poverty, poverty will never be eradicated as long as the private sector is stifled. In the words of Jo' Schwenke, managing director of Business Partners Limited, "We need to remember that the private sector is a lot of individual people; every SME [small and medium enterprise] is built from one entrepreneur."

## *Does Size Matter?*

Even with growing agreement that vibrant private enterprise is essential for vibrant economies, the question remains: Should particular sizes and classes of enterprises be targeted? In the quest to create jobs, reduce poverty, and raise productivity, are equally important roles played by a seamstress making clothes on a sewing machine financed through a microcredit loan, a farmer with fifty employees expanding his business to reach both local and export markets, and hundreds of workers at an automobile plant churning out components for foreign cars?

Rigorous empirical research provides little support for the notion that business size matters for advancing economic growth; instead, the academic literature finds that an enabling environment is critical for healthy enterprises

7. See Ross Levine, "Should Governments and Aid Agencies Subsidize Small Firms?" chapter 5 in this volume.

BOX 1-1
## Microenterprise

Microenterprises are on the front lines of poverty alleviation. Supported by microfinance loans ranging from as little as $50 to as much as $10,000, millions of enterprising poor people worldwide are launching and expanding small restaurants, crafts shops, market stands, and more—and empowering themselves to move from struggling for survival to saving for the future. According to the Consultative Group to Assist the Poor (CGAP), microfinance institutions served more than 80 million clients in 2003. And microfinance's impact on development extends beyond the immediate wage earner, especially when the loan recipient is a woman—because studies show women are most likely to invest in better nutrition, education, and health care for their families.

While microenterprises are individually unlikely to become globally competitive, they are an important means for those at the bottom to climb the rungs of the economic ladder. Success stories abound like that of FINCA client Luz Diamantina Càceres and her husband, whose shoe business grew from a two-person operation that made six dozen pairs of shoes per week to one that employs ten full-time workers and whose output has grown tenfold—thanks to five cycles of microfinance loans totaling $1,650.[1] Thus, while microenterprise may not be the best engine for pathbreaking innovation or capital investment, it is a vital tool for self-employment and lifting the lives and prospects of the poor.

1. FINCA, "Client Stories, Latin America: The Shoemakers," October 2005 (www.villagebanking.org).

of all sizes.[7] But many practitioners nonetheless see important differences between enterprises of various sizes in reducing poverty and promoting innovation and employment. Broadly speaking, practitioners divide enterprises into four classes: microenterprises, small and medium-size enterprises (SMEs), large-scale national enterprises, and huge multinational firms. Microenterprise, while probably not an engine for overall growth, is invaluable for improving the lives of the poorest members of society, as described in box 1-1. SMEs—discussed in box 1-2—can provide bottom-up growth and innovation, while large nationals and multinationals can link local markets to broader, global opportunities, as detailed in box 1-3.

BOX 1-2

**Small and Medium-Size Enterprises**

SMEs (defined here as enterprises with between ten and 100 employees) offer a promising channel for employment, investment, innovation, and growth. In the United States, for example, small businesses provide roughly three out of four of the net new jobs added to the economy.[1] Within SMEs, some enterprises' size and scope may be inherently limited, such as those engaged in the provision of local services (for example, a local construction business). But a potentially critical group of SMEs pursues opportunities for high-yielding investment and innovation that could have a clear multiplier effect on employment, productivity, and growth (for example, a cell phone provider).

1 . U.S. Small Business Administration website.

BOX 1-3

**Large Enterprises and Multinationals**

Large national enterprises and multinationals are critical contributors to capital investment, productivity, and growth. The UN estimates there are more than 60,000 multinational corporations in the world, with hundreds of thousands more foreign affiliates, suppliers, and distributors. Because of their extensive linkages to international trade and capital markets, large firms may offer higher-quality jobs, better pay, and more stability than SMEs, as well as be able to supply foreign markets directly, import technology, and undertake research and development that lead to innovation and productivity improvements. They are also critical conduits linking SMEs and microentrepreneurs to broader market opportunities.

Regardless of whether looking at different sizes of firms constitutes a useful framework for thinking about growth and development, *size definitely matters when it comes to evaluating enterprise needs and constraints*. Financial constraints remain paramount in many poor countries, hitting microenterprises and SMEs particularly hard.

More than two decades of experience have yielded a number of successful models for overcoming the acute constraints that microenterprises initially face (Bhatt and Tang 2001; Brainard 1989). Today, NGOs such as ACCION, FINCA, Unitas, and the Grameen Bank operate effective microlending programs on a large scale with the support of private philanthropy, official donors, and multinational businesses.[8] From Bangladesh to Bolivia, their work has demonstrated that poor people are bankable—indeed, poor clients, especially women, have repayment rates that exceed the formal financial sector in many industrial countries—and also that microfinance institutions can be profitable and self-sustaining.

Such efforts have provided a much-needed impetus for the development of financial intermediaries and other complementary institutions in support of the microfinance sector. One of the goals for 2005, the International Year of Microcredit, was to encourage innovation and strategic partnerships to expand the reach of microfinance to the hundreds of millions of poor people with no bank resources at the bottom of the economic pyramid. One such partnership has been developed between Hewlett-Packard and seven leading microfinance institutions, which have worked together to develop a remote transaction system that effectively turns a microfinance loan officer into a human automated teller machine—thereby reducing cost barriers to microfinance in far-flung rural areas. In some cases, microfinance intermediaries are being transformed from nonprofits to commercial enterprises, although the high transaction costs associated with direct contact with clients suggest a continuing role for philanthropy and public support.

With scalable models for microfinance increasingly well established, attention is shifting to the SME sector, where enterprise needs are more complex and there are fewer successful models. Although SMEs have correspondingly higher needs for capital than microfinance, the problem is not so much the amount as the type of capital needed.

The class of SMEs with the greatest potential for high-yielding investment and innovation is too small and unproven to depend on commercial loans or internal cash flow and simultaneously too large and risky to rely on modest short-term microcredit loans. In sophisticated markets like the United States, a promising business could attract patient risk capital from venture funds or angel investors as well as strategic oversight and management know-how. This sort of financing and support remains virtually nonexistent in most poor countries, in part because of investor concerns about exit risk.

8. FINCA, "Client Stories, Latin America: The Shoemakers."

As a result, developing country entrepreneurs must often struggle to build a business based entirely on their scant personal assets. Or they may be forced to borrow capital and then must pay to service their loan, wiping out any opportunity to invest, take risks, and grow. As the financial practitioners Alan Patricof of Apax Partners and Julie Sunderland have observed, if iconic American firms like Apple Computer, Microsoft, and FedEx had been obliged to finance their early growth with "the short-term, collateralized, high-interest loans currently available in developing countries, they would not even have gotten off the ground."[9]

Promising initiatives are beginning to emerge. Organizations such as Technoserve in Africa and Latin America, Business Partners Limited in South Africa, ShoreBank in the United States, and Enablis in South Africa are pioneering programs to address critical SME needs for financing together with marketing and management advisory services, while the Self-Employed Women's Association in India has launched a Global Trading Network to help microentrepreneurs and SMEs seize global market opportunities. Nourishing this dynamic class of businesses can have a self-reinforcing effect, because successful entrepreneurs serve as employers, trainers, and role models for others.

Clearly, there is no single path to private sector development, and targeting support to one class of enterprise should not mean neglecting the others. That said, SMEs in developing countries are a starved segment with unique potential, and the next few years should see great emphasis on their role as engines of growth and employment.

### *Strengthening Private Investment in Poor Countries*

But how can the capital that indigenous private sectors need to grow be unlocked? And where will the money come from?

Although official aid flows may remain a vital source of financing for a considerable time (particularly for countries with heavy debt burdens), private capital flows already outstrip aid flows for many developing countries and have far greater potential over the medium term. Today, more than $19 trillion is invested in the U.S. securities markets alone. If little more than half of 1 percent of that private capital shifted to investments in developing countries, the increase would radically alter the development landscape. As

9. See Alan Patricof and Julie Sunderland, "Venture Capital for Development," chapter 6 in this volume.

BOX 1-4

### Overcoming Risks Both Real and Perceived

The difficulty of turning around misinformed perceptions is illustrated starkly by Dr. Mohamed Ibrahim, chairman of Celtel International B.V. "I remember the first guy I talked to . . . who designed a number of the networks in Europe and in Asia. I said, 'Let's go and build a telecom network in Uganda.' And he said, 'Mo, are you crazy? There's a guy called Idi Amin in Uganda. Do you want me to drag my company to work in a country run by a crazy guy called Idi Amin?' I said, 'Listen, Idi Amin left 15 years ago.'"[1] Despite these obstacles, Dr. Ibrahim went on to found Celtel International B.V., which now operates cellular networks in 14 countries, serving 6.5 million customers with revenues of $1 billion.

1. Remarks at the Clinton Global Initiative, September 17, 2005.

the social investor Tim Freundlich of the Calvert Social Investment Foundation points out, $100 billion in private capital invested for ten years "could finance 1.14 billion microenterprise jobs, 160 million affordable housing units, and 70 million cooperatives or nonprofit facilities."[10]

Yet getting private investors to bet on poor country markets is a difficult proposition, largely because of perceptions of unacceptably high risk. These perceptions are partly grounded in the reality of political instability, expropriation risk, currency and commodity price swings, and the insufficient legal protections often associated with developing country markets. And such negative perceptions are compounded by a lack of familiarity with developing country environments and inadequate information, financial and otherwise, available to investors who reside on the other side of the world. Capital is notoriously cautious about taking risks—perceived or real. According to some estimates, to offset the perceived risk differential, the expected profitability of a typical SME in a developing country would need to be 50 to 100 percent greater than that of a similar business in a more developed economy (Commonwealth Secretariat 2001). The experience of Celtel in box 1-4 illustrates the extent of the challenge.

10. See Timothy Freundlich, "Blended Value Investment and a Living Return," chapter 4 in this volume.

BOX 1-5

**Global Development Bonds**

One important goal is to magnify aggregate private flows into poor countries by attracting commercial and institutional investors. The most promising approach might be to satisfy these investors' fiduciary responsibility to invest conservatively through the adaptation of sophisticated financial techniques originally developed for rich country capital markets. A group of experienced business executives, economists, and government experts is currently developing a promising concept called Global Development Bonds (GDB), which seek to boost development capital abroad much as the municipal bond market has done for states and localities at home. While some official support would be required, the GDB architects underscore that the goal is to have a market product supported by the government, not the other way round.

Diaspora communities can be mobilized to support development in their ancestral homelands, as Ireland, China, and India have shown. Some African countries are attempting to learn from these successes by identifying and tapping into their far-flung diasporas.

Leaders of poor countries can and must make a difference by implementing effective policies. But achieving an attractive environment for private enterprise is a long-term endeavor that requires sustained political will, patience, and not inconsiderable luck.

In the meantime, changing risk perceptions and reward expectations for investments in development will require official donors and lenders, NGOs, and private investors to exercise greater creativity in designing or adapting mechanisms to mitigate risk, building on the wide variety of tools and techniques available in the most sophisticated financial markets. One innovative new approach is the concept of Global Development Bonds, described in box 1-5. In considering what kinds of new financing options to develop, the place to begin is with the problem to be addressed and the goal to be achieved, as Brookings scholar David de Ferranti points out.[11]

11. See David de Ferranti, "Innovative Financing Options and the Fight against Global Poverty: What's New and What Next," chapter 7 in this volume.

There is already considerable experience with different forms of official guarantees provided by organizations such as the World Bank Group's International Finance Corporation and the U.S. Overseas Private Investment Corporation on a case-by-case basis. But these approaches have often proven laborious and time consuming for willing investors to use; a goal for these institutions should be to move from "tailor-made" to "off-the-shelf" products wherever possible. As Richard Blum, chairman of Blum Capital Partners, notes, "People go to an official finance institution for investment guarantees, and they're two years older by the time they're done. The difficulty of the process is a disincentive to potential investors. Official finance institutions need to develop easy to understand programs and guidelines. They have to move from the tailor made to the ready made business."

The public sector has also helped to establish and subsidize venture funds focused on investments in transitional and developing economies. The Polish-American Enterprise Fund was an early success, and the European Bank for Reconstruction and Development has subsequently launched a variety of funds for the former Soviet Union. But these venture funds usually have not met expectations, and many funds originally intended to support SMEs have drifted toward bigger deals, in the face of high SME transaction costs and the pressure to produce commercial returns. There is an ongoing debate over the use of equity relative to debt in providing financing for SMEs, as discussed in box 1-6.

Inevitably, there will be tough challenges and trade-offs in setting up these new efforts. Some experts question whether using public funds to support the private sector is the best use of limited resources for poverty alleviation. How do we measure whether a dollar is better invested in a girl's education or in building the business that will provide that girl with a livelihood as an entrepreneur or an employee? Others point to the danger of distorting the market with too much cheap capital or support for uncompetitive businesses. Will government guarantees lead to lax project assessments and poor investment decisions? Will funders have the courage to cut off underperforming clients?

In addition, there is tension between the desire to reduce transaction costs for developing country investments and the recognition that technical assistance can be as important as, if not more important than, finance for many ventures. Many organizations provide financial support in combination with strategic advice and business skills development to help promising entrepreneurs reach their fullest potential. Yet the more features that are added to a program, the more costly it becomes to replicate and scale. Recognizing this,

BOX 1-6
### SME Finance: Equity or Debt?

An objective is to direct patient investment capital to the hungry SME sector. While accepting the need for lower returns or subsidies due to the high transaction costs, there is still considerable debate on whether long-term loans or equity are better suited to address SME financing needs.

Alan Patricof and Julie Sunderland propose a venture capital fund to invest equity or equity-like instruments in growth-oriented SMEs in poor countries. The fund would combine resources from development financial institutions, local governments, and private local investors. Most of the investors would accept a below-market rate of return in the hopes of leveraging and building the indigenous commercial risk capital market.[1]

In contrast, Jo' Schwenke of Business Partners Limited has pioneered a model built around long-term loans. In his words, "It's not about equity, it's about attitude. If a business is in trouble and you foreclose, that's thinking like a banker. If you stick it out, that's thinking like an entrepreneur. The problem with an equity deal is that if you take the fair share you need, your entrepreneur will start thinking like an employee."

So far, the lending approach is getting more of a test run. The Shell Foundation recently teamed up with African-based specialist financier GroFin to launch a $100 million loan fund for small business investments in Africa, funded mainly by the U.K. and Dutch governments and two African banks. But going forward, both equity and lending approaches should be put to the test.

1. See chapter by Patricof and Sunderland in this volume.

some are devising creative approaches to providing technical assistance on a not-for-profit basis while offering financial support at closer to market terms.

Finally, some experts believe these efforts are misguided, noting that history is littered with failed attempts to finance the private sector in developing countries—from directed credit to development banks. They believe that the maximum development impact is more likely to be gained by supporting macroeconomic policy change than by trying to provide financial support directly to private enterprises. However, many earlier efforts failed because the government tried to play the role of the capital market without enforcing market discipline or demanding returns. The new generation of innovative financing approaches aims to put market discipline at the core, with an emphasis on performance and accountability. Far from supplanting market mechanisms, the goal of new risk-sharing tools is to create appropriate incentives for private investors to venture into markets they would otherwise write off as hopeless.

The time has come to turn more of these ideas into reality and give them a test run—with close collaboration among official donors, NGOs, and experienced financial market players. Rather than seeking a silver bullet, those committed to spurring development should pursue a range of promising endeavors.

## The Business of Poverty Reduction: The Global Private Sector's Role

From the classroom to the boardroom, debates have long been under way about the appropriate role for business and its responsibility to society. One school of thought follows Milton Friedman's view that corporate executives, provided they stay within the law, have no business responsibilities beyond making as much money for their shareholders as they can. Another school argues that corporations are social institutions and have an obligation to lift lives and livelihoods in the places in which they do business—or, at a minimum, to do no harm. That obligation increasingly has global dimensions.

The issue has moved well beyond abstract discussion, as greater awareness on the part of consumers, investors, and workers—along with the increased presence of transnational NGOs and the interest of the media—has put corporate practices under the microscope. In an age when civic activists are quick to point out that the annual revenues of many global firms dwarf the gross domestic products of the world's poorest nations, modern businesses find themselves scrutinized not just on their profitability but also on their broader social, environmental, and human rights impact. Moreover, the same tools of globalization that have enabled companies to grow have been used by corporate critics to launch sophisticated campaigns against firms perceived as falling short on the social front. Today more than ever, good corporate citizenship is tied to the bottom line.

In response, many companies have adopted corporate social responsibility approaches that seek to mitigate negative social and environmental consequences through adherence to minimum standards. Many multinationals have agreed to comply with voluntary standards and corporate codes of conduct in areas such as labor protection, transparency of resource flows, and environmental stewardship in poor countries.

Increasingly, these codes are being negotiated in international forums, such as the UN's Global Compact, which now involves almost 2,000 companies worldwide. Some are being made operational through multilateral institutions. For instance, the World Bank's Equator Principles encourage the world's leading financial institutions to incorporate social and environmental considerations into large infrastructure projects.

Pressure is mounting to give these codes teeth through regular audits and third-party monitoring in industries such as apparel and footwear. Although some corporations have been reluctant to embrace these enhanced approaches, a few industry leaders such as Nike have progressed well beyond basic compliance to develop an elaborate and now transparent set of supply chain management practices to ensure robust implementation.

Indeed, some top executives themselves would argue that the scope of corporate social responsibility is too narrow—to the detriment of business and society alike. As Ian Davis, the worldwide managing director of McKinsey & Company, has written, these kinds of commitments are "too limited, too defensive and too disconnected from corporate strategy."[12] Visionary corporate leaders are revising the definition of business value beyond pure shareholder value—or are looking beyond the horizon where the two converge—seeking to proactively manage their corporations' social footprint as a fundamental part of strategic planning.

This growing movement to build social values into core business strategies can have a transformative impact on development and poverty. At the same time, it can bring real benefits to companies—including improving customer loyalty and employee morale and helping to refine brand identity. It is not simply a matter of responsibility but also more and more of opportunity.

Three angles in particular merit exploration: how to think about the private sector's contribution to development, what can be done to maximize the effectiveness of public-private partnerships, and what can be learned from the private sector's mobilization in the global health arena.

### *The Private Sector's Development Footprint*

The development footprint of corporations ranges from their core business activities to their philanthropic activities to their policy and advocacy activities and increasingly is reaching into a realm where social value and market value converge.

12. Ian Davis, "The Biggest Contract," *Economist,* May 28, 2005, p. 88.

***Core Business Activities.*** Perhaps the most important and still least recognized potential opportunity for businesses to influence development is through their core business activities—from what and how they sell to how they operate and to the challenges they take on.

For example, many businesses are engaged in creating social value by addressing the underserved needs of poor consumers within the traditional for-profit model. Indeed, the business scholar C. K. Prahalad has drawn attention to "the fortune at the bottom of the pyramid"—the vast market potential associated with the billions of consumers who survive on less than $2 a day (Prahalad 2005, p. 24). As Prahalad argues, poor consumers have both choice and dignity—something that is easy to forget when they are viewed solely through the lens of charity. Indeed, poor people are some of the most value-conscious consumers in the world.

Pioneering firms from Brazil to India are finding new ways to address this huge market's underserved needs—from selling individual sachets of shampoo to creating a systematized and standardized eye-care process that allows a doctor and two technician teams to perform more than fifty cataract surgeries a day. The challenge for businesses attempting to serve this market is to develop appropriate products, marketing, and distribution—meaning "small unit packages, low margin per unit, high volume, and high return on capital employed" (Prahalad 2005, p. 24).

Other corporations are delivering important development benefits through their core business activities in poor countries by developing human resources, building infrastructure, and introducing new technologies. In the words of former Overseas Private Investment Corporation chairman Peter Watson, "The most valuable contribution of foreign investment does not come from the addition to the domestic pool of capital and the creation of jobs per se, but from the transfer of globally competitive technologies and business practices"—such as quality control procedures, time management, project management skills, and experience in handling external relationships.[13]

The next frontier may be for businesses to deploy their core competencies against tough development challenges—as will be discussed below in the context of partnerships and of health. Enterprises that have passed the market test on a global scale often have world-class capabilities in areas that are of great importance and short supply in the development field. These include

13. Peter Watson, "Private Sector Investment in Development," Brookings Blum Roundtable, July 2004.

capabilities in research and development, as well as marketing, and successfully adapting business models to vastly differing markets while driving down costs.

*Corporate Philanthropy.* Corporations have traditionally viewed their positive development impact primarily through the lens of philanthropic activities in local communities—such as supporting education and youth development projects, building community leaders' capacity, training local specialists in environmental management, and establishing microcredit programs. Companies may give financial resources, offer employee volunteers, donate materials and equipment, or even provide space. These efforts can often be leveraged through partnerships with local NGOs and businesses, the host government, and official donors.

The potential reach of corporate philanthropy is huge. In Jane Nelson's estimation, the philanthropic resources of the top fifty companies equal the United Nations Development Program's annual operating budget of $4 billion.[14] Visionary companies are starting to think about philanthropy in strategic terms—making longer-term, holistic commitments to communities rather than a series of individual, one-time donations. At the same time, there are challenges involved in fully leveraging corporate philanthropy's development promise; big firms may be reluctant to pool resources with competitors or to work with partners if it means sharing the public relations credit.

*Policy Dialogue and Advocacy.* Another important channel for leveraging business influence is through policy dialogue and advocacy—such as business pressure to improve the climate for private firms in poor countries and corporate lobbying in support of more development aid or enhanced market access for poor countries. One such effort was launched in 2003, when a group of business leaders in Seattle joined forces to advocate on behalf of the world's poor. Bill Gates Sr., Daniel J. Evans, Bill Ruckelshaus, Bill Clapp, and John Shalikashvili founded the Initiative for Global Development (IGD) as an alliance of business and civic leaders dedicated to reducing extreme global poverty. Starting from its roots in Seattle, IGD has expanded to ten cities across the United States, with plans for further national outreach.

Increasingly, private, public, and nonprofit partners are joining forces on behalf of shared goals. For instance, business and civil society are natural allies in the fight against corruption, which, by strangling trust, hinders

14. See Jane Nelson, chapter 3 in this volume.

investment and enterprise as well as effective government. BP and Shell have teamed up with NGOs such as the Open Society Institute, Global Witness, and Transparency International in partnerships such as Publish What You Pay and the Extractive Industries Transparency Initiative that use the power of transparency to lift the "resource curse" of dysfunctional governments and predatory elites that too often afflict countries rich in natural resources. In the words of Nigerian finance minister Ngozi Okonjo-Iweala, "We are publishing the oil revenues by each tier of government in the newspapers every month. Believe me, it's the most popular reform because people can say to their local government chairman or their state governor, 'You got X amount of Naira, 20 billion, why are our roads not fixed?'"[15]

*Marrying Social Value and Market Value.* On a parallel track, innovative ventures such as the Acumen Fund are marrying philanthropy with commercial savvy to invest venture capital in developing country enterprises that can provide health, housing, water, and other basic services to poor people in a sustainable, scalable way. These hybrid approaches place a premium on generating social value, but they have the potential to generate profits over the longer term. Promising areas for hybrid ventures include agribio, health, and clean energy.

Another cutting-edge approach is "blended value investing," which argues for a redefinition of market returns to incorporate social and environmental value. This type of investing is still at a relatively early stage of evolution and will require advances in social and environmental accounting as well as the creation of supporting institutions to achieve scale. But growing numbers of investors already are expressing the desire to create social value when allocating their portfolios—whether through strategies to limit investment in companies that pollute the environment or exploit their workers or through proactive investments that accept below-market returns in exchange for enhanced social value.

In sum, numerous avenues exist for the global private sector to help create social value. But the path ahead is neither clear nor easy. There is often a difficult tension between long-term development goals for poor people and corporations' short-term pressures to deliver shareholder profits. What then will it take to channel the power of private enterprise in these directions? How can society create conditions for the private sector to do the right thing?

15. Remarks at the Clinton Global Initiative, September 17, 2005.

Given that business continues, appropriately, to be motivated by financial returns, one key requirement is to demonstrate that failure to focus adequately on social impact can ultimately reduce a corporation's strategic options or, conversely, that social value and market value converge over time—as Starbucks is doing by demonstrating that consumers are willing to pay premium prices for a business system that invests in its suppliers and employees.

Perceived public relations benefits or costs also influence corporate decisionmaking. The more that the media, NGOs, civil society, and shareholders reward the reputations of socially responsible corporations and their leaders—and tarnish those of offenders—the more incentives firms will have to burnish their corporate citizenship credentials.

Similarly, companies value the connections emerging between doing good in the community and building employee satisfaction. For example, the executives of Voxiva, a for-profit data solutions provider that uses technology to address public health needs in poor countries, believe their emphasis on doing good and doing well at the same time has been an asset in attracting and retaining highly motivated employees (Prahalad 2005). And some jewelers who were targets of the "Clean Diamonds" campaign reported that they felt the biggest loss not on their bottom line but in employee morale (Rosen 2003). With more MBA programs focusing attention on social enterprise and corporate citizenship, tomorrow's top recruits may hold out for jobs that offer meaning as well as money.

### *Realizing the Full Potential of Public-Private Partnerships*

As multinationals and large-scale national enterprises embrace a broader mission, many are seeking ways to leverage their resources through partnerships with local NGOs and businesses, host governments, and official donors. For many large companies, working with official donors bestows a range of advantages. Donor involvement can often confer legitimacy on corporate social responsibility efforts such as product trademarks or natural resource transparency programs. When corporations work to promote social value in areas related to their core business proposition, such as on social marketing efforts, they may enter into partnership with governments to support marketing and distribution targeted at the poorest consumers. And when corporations seek to contribute to social welfare in the poor communities where they do business, partnerships with host governments and official donors ensure synergy with broader development plans and programs.

Moreover, public sector partners can help corporations gain policy access to governments, provide convening authority, mitigate risk, and share significant accumulated expertise in developing countries. Often, firms investing in developing countries seek the involvement of the official, multilateral International Finance Corporation—not primarily for financial reasons, but rather because it conveys an official stamp of approval with regard to environmental and social standards.

Likewise, official donors increasingly value public-private joint ventures. During the past few decades, as aid agencies have shifted from viewing the local private sector as a target for development to looking to the private sector for social service delivery and infrastructure provision, governments have grown to rely on the private sector's significant project management expertise, established local presence, and valuable political support.

Although many assume that the public sector is seeking to leverage financing from corporations, in reality governments often serve as the "resource" partner, seeking to leverage the private sector's know-how and commitment. Thus, for instance, when Hewlett-Packard collaborated with the U.S. Agency for International Development and several leading NGOs to develop technology for microfinance operations, it was the government—not the private sector—that supplied the money, while Hewlett-Packard provided project management skills, personnel, and technology.

The United States has long been prominent in these efforts, in keeping with the dominant domestic role of its private sector and the abundance of American-based corporations with global reach. But European business leaders, such as the global banking group ABN AMRO, have been taking the lead on partnerships with governments and civil society organizations to advance social responsibility—an area from which the U.S. government has mostly remained aloof. Among international institutions, the World Bank has traditionally had an outsized role in private sector development, with the United Nations Development Program making big strides in recent years.

Yet for all this activity, challenges remain in maximizing these partnerships' potential. In the corporate world, it has been estimated that roughly half of strategic alliances underperform or fail. The public-private partnership arena faces similar hurdles.

At the most basic level, public-private partnerships must overcome cultural clashes. Corporations may feel that government collaboration weighs down their agility and makes projects hard to scale, while official donors may feel that their reliance on public funds, and procedural concerns about fairness and due process, makes it difficult to grant shared responsibility to a corporate partner. Multilateral institutions are further hamstrung by national rivalries among member states, which may lead one country to resist another's firms receiving public sector support.

In addition, many donor agencies view public-private partnerships "almost exclusively in terms of corporate social responsibility and/or as a marginal supplement to their other programs for promoting private sector growth," according to Larry Cooley, the president of Management Systems International.[16] As a result, their partnership offices are often understaffed and lack bureaucratic clout. The U.S. Agency for International Development, however, has integrated public-private partnerships across its development efforts—and has taken commensurate measures to fund and train staff as well as change relevant operational and procurement procedures to foster the use of this business model. Similarly, corporations that strongly value strategic alliances place a premium on designating and retaining good people to manage these relationships over time. In the words of Bill Ruckelshaus of Madrona Ventures Fund, "Some companies make it their livelihood to make strategic partnerships work. Many of the same principles are transferable to partnerships with the public sector. These include time up front to structure the partnership, which is invaluable: exit strategies, establishing common interests and understanding shared goals, with periodic review to make sure that people are on the same page. Often these dry issues, if ignored, are what make partnerships break up."

Another key challenge is misaligned expectations among various parties to a partnership—from the motives for undertaking a partnership in the first place to expectations about the pace of decisionmaking and resource allocation. To avoid this problem, both sides need to agree early in the project design process on what each side hopes to gain from the endeavor and who will bring what to the table. Open communication, transparency, clarity of roles and ground rules, and regular opportunities for review can help get a partnership going and keep it moving forward. Just as important is mutual agreement on an appropriate exit strategy in case the alliance outlives its utility. Time invested in the planning stages of a partnership can pay important dividends, and save disappointment, down the line.

In the coming years, a well-tested set of best practices should help guide public-private partnerships in achieving their full potential—including ways to scale good programs, replicate successful configurations, and exit gracefully

16. See Larry Cooley, "2 + 2 = 5: A Pragmatic View of Partnerships between Official Donors and Multinational Corporations," chapter 8 in this volume.

from bad ones. It already seems clear that certain sectors are better suited for these partnerships than others—among them health, water, natural resource industries, and information technology education.

And as forward-looking business leaders increasingly broaden their definitions of value creation, and government executives grow to appreciate the operational savvy and local presence that private partners can bring, public-private partnerships are bound to grow in reach and impact. Though development and poverty reduction primarily remain challenges for governments, effective partnerships are proving every day that corporations can be capable, creative allies.

### *Learning from Success: Advances in Health*

Nowhere is the proof of public-private partnerships' potential more compelling than in the health arena. Defying development pessimists, global health has witnessed some dramatic successes in recent decades. Unlike economic interventions, which are highly dependent on context for their success, many health interventions have been effectively implemented—even in countries with dysfunctional governments, poor public health systems, and civil conflict.

Improved sanitation, combined with inexpensive oral rehydration therapy, helped to achieve a two-thirds drop in deaths from diarrheal disease between 1980 and 1999. And in one of the biggest triumphs of science and political will, smallpox has been completely eradicated—and polio is well on its way to disappearing. Today, the World Health Organization estimates that it is possible to eradicate measles—the single leading cause of death among Africa's children—through vaccinations costing only 26 cents a child.

The successes with polio and smallpox are instructive in other ways as well. In both cases, the immunizations already existed, pulled along by rich country demand. In contrast, encouraging spending on research and development and expensive clinical trials for poor country disease treatments that are not likely to ever be profitable presents a singular predicament for policymakers. According to the Global Forum for Health Research, only 10 percent of global medical research is devoted to diseases that cause 90 percent of the world's health burden.[17] And of the more than 1,200 drugs that reached the market between 1975 and 1997, a scant thirteen were intended for treatment of tropical infectious diseases in developing countries.

17. Global Health Forum, "Helping Correct the 10/90 Gap" (www.globalforumhealth.org/Site/003__The%2010%2090%20gap/001__Now.php [May 31, 2006]).

Public-private partnerships are beginning to turn those statistics around. A report from the London School of Economics and Political Science found that between 2000 and 2004, public-private partnerships invested $112 million to stimulate research on ten neglected diseases, including malaria, tuberculosis, and leprosy.[18] As a result, more than sixty new drug research projects are under way, with the potential for half a dozen new drugs being registered by 2010. In the words of Chris Hentschel, the chief executive of the Medicines for Malaria Venture, "In our Public Private Partnership for Health there are 80 products in the pipeline. We aim to have drugs become instantly generic, while companies retain the rights to a small profitable market. This is mostly dependent on philanthropy—however, the tsunami showed that people don't mind having their money spent on these things."

There is simply no substitute for the private sector's research and development capacity in medicines, but it will not be deployed for poor country diseases on the basis of anticipated profits. The Brookings and Harvard scholar Michael Kremer has put forth the powerful proposal that public and philanthropic funding should provide incentives to pharmaceutical and biotechnology companies by mimicking the market—offering guaranteed purchase commitments for successfully tested vaccines and disease treatments—which has evolved into an actionable policy proposal termed Advance Purchase Commitments (Glennerster and Kremer 2000).

For diseases where rich country demand has already created profitable investment opportunities, the challenge is to make the resulting drugs available in poor countries at affordable prices. The late Brookings and University of California, Berkeley, scholar Jean Lanjouw proposed that pharmaceutical companies allow generic versions of their drugs to be produced for the poorest countries without requiring royalties (Lanjouw 2001). Under her proposal, pharmaceutical companies would lose nothing because these markets are unprofitable anyway, while the poorest countries would gain access to life-saving drugs at close to cost. Turning this proposal into reality, however, will require not only securing the active support of pharmaceutical companies concerned about the erosion of intellectual property rights but also enlisting generic producers in developing countries, recipient governments, and official and philanthropic donors.

The growing list of innovative global health initiatives, including those detailed in boxes 1-7 and 1-8, demonstrates the power of the private sector to

18. London School of Economics, *The New Landscape of Neglected Disease Drug Development,* Pharmaceutical R&D Policy Project (www.lse.ac.uk/collections/pressandinformation office/PDF/Neglected_Diseases_05.pdf [May 31, 2006]).

BOX 1-7

**Partnering to Deploy Vaccines for Poor Children**

The dynamic public-private Global Alliance for Vaccines and Immunizations (GAVI) is pioneering important innovations in both the financing and delivery of public health in poor countries. Established to bring new vaccines and improve immunization systems in the poorest countries, GAVI secured in September 2005 a $4 billion International Finance Facility for Immunization (IFFIm) that will leverage long-term donor funding commitments through borrowing in private capital markets. Initial pledges have come from the United Kingdom, France, Italy, Spain, Sweden, and the Gates Foundation. The large scale of financing and its predictability will enable GAVI and its poor country partners to engage in longer-term immunization system improvements and purchasing contracts. GAVI estimates the IFFIm resources will save the lives of more than 5 million children over the next decade.[1]

1. See chapter by Shah and Mathews in this volume.

address social challenges when it teams up with private philanthropy, official donors, NGOs, and local authorities.[19] These initiatives also provide a fascinating case study of how the strategies of pharmaceutical companies have evolved as they have found themselves on the front lines of the global poverty debate. Though some companies remain wedded to a narrow shareholder-value approach, others have embraced social responsibility and employed philanthropy and partnerships to advance social welfare.

## Answering the Call to Action

In many respects, the world's track record on development is disheartening. Someone born in Zambia today has less likelihood of reaching the age of thirty than someone born in England in 1840. Eighteen countries have seen declines in the quality of human development since 1990.

Yet there is cause for hope. With visionary leadership, the world community can turn the tide. The *Human Development Report 2005* challenges governments to "show that they mean business." The private sector, too, must

19. See Rajiv Shah and Sylvia Mathews, "Financing for Global Health," chapter 9 in this volume.

BOX 1-8
**Partnering to Eradicate Polio**

An innovative partnership of the Gates Foundation, the World Bank, Rotary International, and the UN Foundation deploys performance-based buy-downs of World Bank loans to encourage poor countries to pursue the final stages of polio eradication. Nigeria and Pakistan have already taken advantage of this program; India and a number of African countries are interested as well. The initiative could help close the gap between the enormous social value of complete global polio eradication and the unattractive cost-benefit calculation faced by poor country governments, which incur steep costs and only modest benefits from addressing the very last cases.

step up to the plate—not just as a matter of conscience, but also because businesses cannot hope to thrive in countries and communities that fail. A clear call to action emerges from the yawning gulf between today's heartrending reality and the promise inherent in our unprecedented resources and scientific and technological capacities.

Private enterprise is a powerful engine for transforming the development landscape. Forward-looking executives are weaving social and environmental goals into their core business strategies. Top corporations are banding together in groups like the International Business Leaders Forum and the Business Leaders Initiative for Human Rights, joined by an explicit commitment to build a better, more equitable world. World-class business schools are stepping up the prominence of corporate social responsibility in their curricula. Development experts in government, civil society, and the philanthropic arena are devising new ways to join forces and resources with private sector partners.

Helping poor people is a smart investment in the future all people are destined to share. In this interconnected world, no society can advance as long as most of humanity is left behind. That is simply common sense—and more than ever, business sense as well.

Today's dynamic, value-driven private sector has the ability, incentive, and duty to act. The dream of development is within reach.

## References

Bhatt, Nitin, and Shui-Yan Tang. 2001. "Delivering Microfinance in Developing Countries: Controversies and Policy Perspectives." *Policy Studies Journal* 29 (no. 2): 319–34.

Brainard, Lael. 1989. "Senegal Community and Enterprise Development Project: Achieving Viability." In *Seeking Solutions: Framework and Cases for Small Enterprise Development Programs*, edited by Charles Mann, Merilee Grindle, and Parker Shipton. Hartford, Conn.: Kumarian Press.

Commonwealth Secretariat. 2001. *Lowering the Threshold: Changing Private Investors' Perceptions by Reducing the Cost and Risk of Investment in Least Developed, Small and Vulnerable Economies*. London.

Glennerster, Rachel, and Michael Kremer. 2000. *A World Bank Vaccine Commitment*. Brookings Policy Brief 57, May.

Klein, Michael, and Bita Hadjimichael. 2003. *The Private Sector in Development: Entrepreneurship, Regulation, and Competitive Disciplines*. Washington, D.C.: World Bank.

Lanjouw, Jean O. 2001. *A Patent Policy Proposal for Global Diseases*. Brookings Policy Brief 87, June.

Porter, Michael. 2004. *Microeconomic Foundations of Competitiveness: The Policy Agenda for Developing Countries*. Washington, D.C.: Center for Strategic and International Studies.

Prahalad, C. K. 2005. *The Fortune at the Bottom of the Pyramid: Eradicating Poverty through Profits*. Philadelphia: Wharton School Publishing.

Rosen, Irwin. 2003. "Corporate Social Investment and Branding in the New South Africa." *Journal of Brand Management* 10, nos. 4–5 (May).

United Nations Commission on the Private Sector and Development. 2004. *Unleashing Entrepreneurship: Making Business Work for the Poor*. New York.

World Bank. 2004a. *Doing Business in 2004: Understanding Regulation*. Washington, D.C.

———. 2004b. *World Development Report 2005: A Better Investment Climate for Everyone*. Oxford University Press.

———. 2005. *Doing Business in 2005: Removing Obstacles to Growth*. Washington, D.C.

———. 2006. *Doing Business in 2006: Creating Jobs*. Washington, D.C.

# 2

# *Unleashing Entrepreneurship*

Warrick Smith

Today, few informed commentators question that the private sector plays a critical role in growth and poverty reduction. The ideological debates of the past are giving way to more pragmatic discussions about how best to unleash and expand that contribution while preserving other social values. New research is also providing fresh insights into what works and what does not. Many developing countries are making huge strides in acting on this agenda and achieving dramatic reductions in poverty as a result. China and India provide the most dramatic examples, but important successes can also be seen in countries as diverse as Latvia, Uganda, Vietnam, and El Salvador.

This chapter presents a brief overview of what we have learned about the role of private sector development in growth and poverty reduction, and it highlights the central role of government policies and behaviors in influencing the size of that contribution.

## Entrepreneurship, Growth, and Poverty Reduction

When we think of "entrepreneurs" in the U.S. context, we often conjure up images of a young(er) Bill Gates heading toward his first million, or perhaps

Warrick Smith is a manager for policy and strategy in the World Bank Group's Private Sector Development Vice Presidency. Before joining the World Bank as a private sector development specialist in 1993, Smith held a number of senior positions in the Australian government, including secretary of a major independent review of competition policy, lead adviser on international trade and investment law, and director responsible for resource trade issues. He studied economics and law at the Australian National University before completing a master's in public administration at Harvard University's Kennedy School of Government.

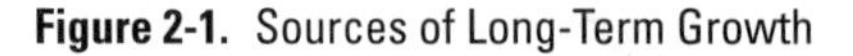

**Figure 2-1.** Sources of Long-Term Growth

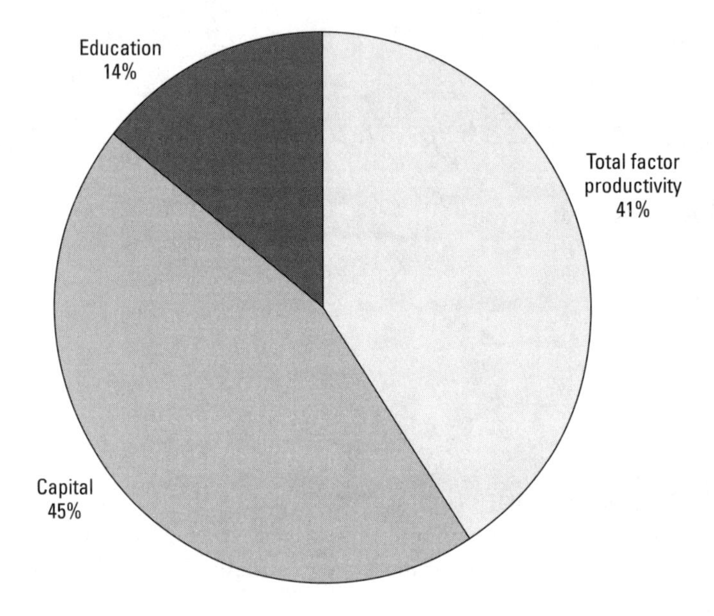


a range of successful businesspeople taking on significant risks in pursuit of greater rewards. Surely, they meet the test. But when assessing the contribution of entrepreneurship to development, we need a more all-encompassing view. We need to include peasant farmers toiling in their fields in Uganda and Bangladesh; street vendors peddling their wares in La Paz and Manila; and microenterprises in Cairo and Istanbul. There are small manufacturing concerns, restaurants, and florists. Even less romantically, perhaps, we also need to recognize that large and foreign enterprises can make a significant contribution to growth and poverty reduction in developing countries.

How does such a diverse group of actors, driven by the quest for profit, contribute to growth and poverty reduction? Let us begin with economic growth, which is now understood to be critical to a sustained improvement in living standards. Aggregate-level evidence shows that the key drivers of long-term growth are investment and productivity improvements (figure 2-1). The private sector is the principal source of investment, with domestic private investment substantially overshadowing foreign investment across the developing world (figure 2-2). Though the relationship between investment and productivity can be difficult to disentangle, the evidence confirms the

**Figure 2-2.** Domestic Private Investment and Foreign Direct Investment (FDI) in Developing Countries

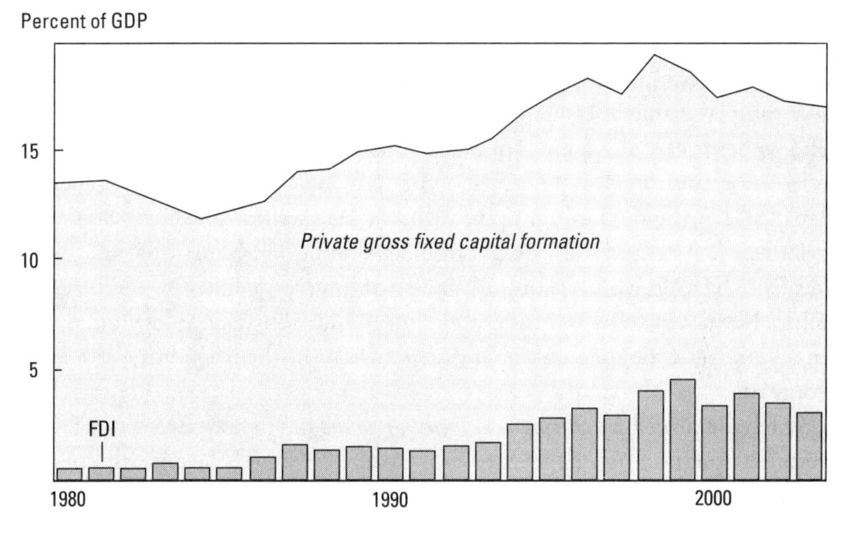


Source: World Development Indicators.

powerful role competition plays in driving productivity improvement in a process that Joseph Schumpeter famously referred to as "creative destruction."

How do investment and productivity improvements translate into poverty reduction? The most obvious mechanism is job creation. The private sector accounts for about 90 percent of jobs in developing countries, and poor people rate self-employment and jobs as the two most promising ways to improve their situation. But employment is not the only mechanism. A vibrant private sector expands the availability and reduces the prices of goods in society, including goods consumed by poor people. And firms and commercial transactions are the main source of taxes from which governments can empower poor people through investments in health, education, and other public goods, as well as through direct income transfers.

## Entrepreneurship and the Investment Climate

Firms and entrepreneurs invest and make productivity improvements not out of any sense of philanthropy but to make profits. Their decisions are thus influenced by the expected risks and rewards associated with alternative courses of action. Those risks and rewards are in turn shaped by the investment climate, which supplies the opportunities and incentives to invest productively, create jobs, and expand. But what shapes the investment climate?

A substantial body of research has looked at the role of *geography*—including natural resource endowments, climate, and market size. Though such factors can play a role, they are rarely decisive. For example, substantial resource endowments can prove more of a curse than a blessing when they lead societies to be consumed by rent seeking or civil conflict, and countries such as Japan and Singapore have prospered with limited natural resources. Similarly, relatively small and remote economies, including Mauritius and New Zealand, have grown by taking advantage of international trade. More generally, advances in transportation and communications technology are doing much to overcome the tyranny of distance, not only between but also within countries.

The role played by *culture* and *social attitudes* has also attracted significant research attention. At the level of individuals, we know that investment and other decisions do not always conform to the presumed "rational actor" model of traditional economics. For example, people tend to be loss averse—more willing to accept risk to avoid a loss than to realize a gain of the same size. Similarly, attitudes toward risk taking, innovation, and proactivity vary between individuals in any society and possibly between societies as well. The latter can be shaped by a range of factors, including traditions and related social institutions. But even these influences are not immutable, with attitudes and related institutions evolving in response to new experiences and new information, including the demonstration effects provided by successful entrepreneurs.

Although geography and social attitudes are difficult to change over at least the short run, governments have far more decisive influence over their own policies and behaviors. And new research highlights the critical role *government policies and behaviors* play in shaping the investment climate and hence the private sector's contribution to growth and poverty reduction. Relevant policies and behaviors cover a broad terrain, including stability and security (including the security of property rights); regulation and taxation, both at and within a country's borders; the adequacy of basic infrastructure; the functioning of finance markets; workers' skills and the operation of labor markets; and broader governance features, including corruption. Policies and behaviors in these areas influence the investment climate via the risks, costs, and barriers to competition faced by firms.

**Figure 2-3.** Concerns of Firms in Developing Countries

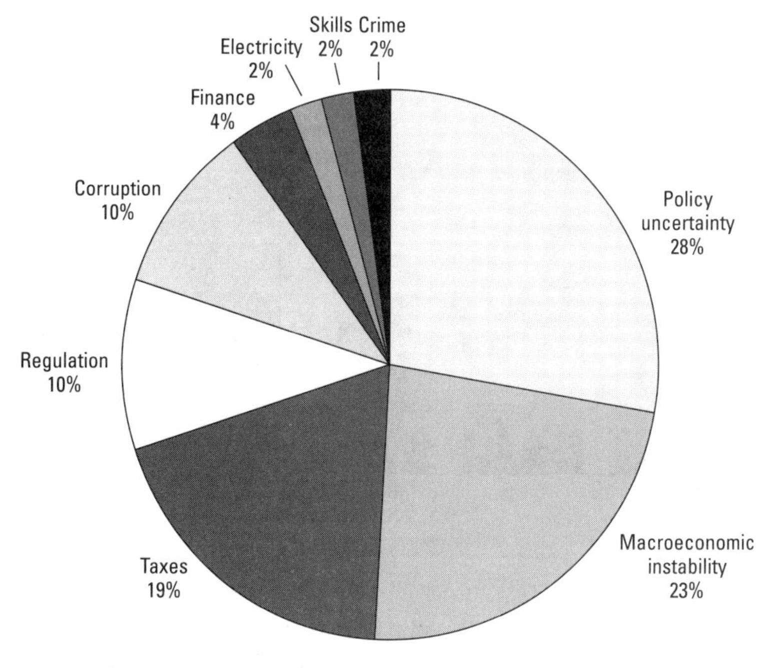


Source: World Bank survey data.

## Reducing Risks, Costs, and Barriers to Competition

Because investment is forward looking, *risks* play a critical role in shaping investment behavior. Though some risks are inherent in any commercial endeavor—such as the risk that customers will prefer the products of competitors—many are directly influenced by government. Indeed, surveys undertaken by the World Bank show that policy-related risk (particularly policy uncertainty and macroeconomic instability) dominates the concerns of firms in developing countries (figure 2-3). The World Bank's work also suggests that improving policy certainty alone could increase the likelihood of new investment by more than 30 percent.

The surveys also show large variations in the level of individual risks perceived between countries. For example, 90 percent of firms in Guatemala reported that the interpretation of regulation was unpredictable, but fewer than one-third of firms in China reported the same. Confidence in the courts

**Figure 2-4.** Taxes Are Often Just the Tip of the Iceberg

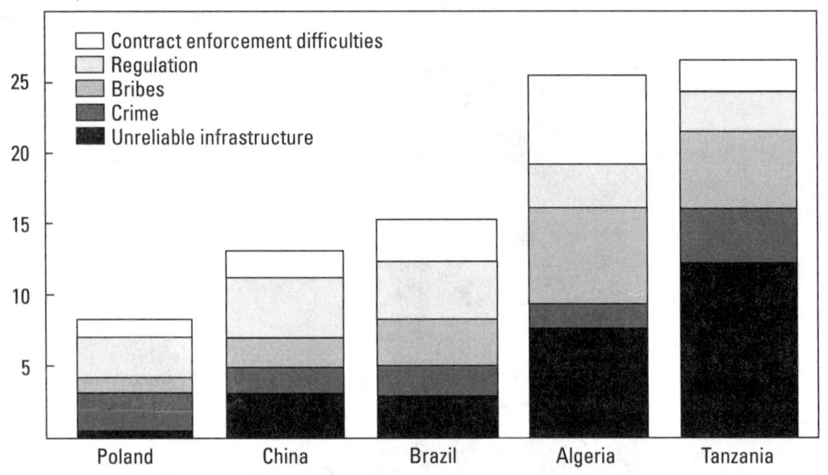


Source: World Bank Investment Climate Surveys.

to enforce contracts also varied widely, with more than 80 percent of firms in Bangladesh reporting a lack of confidence but fewer than 20 percent of firms in Malaysia doing so.

### *Costs*

Government policies and behaviors influence the level of costs faced by firms and hence the range of opportunities that might potentially be profitable. Though firms in every country complain about taxes, the survey data show that taxes are rarely the biggest obstacle. Indeed, in some countries poor infrastructure, burdensome regulation, contract enforcement difficulties, crime, and corruption can amount to more than 25 percent of sales—or more than three times what firms typically pay in taxes (figure 2-4).

The World Bank's Doing Business project also highlights huge variations in regulatory compliance costs across countries. Registering a new business takes 2 days in Australia, but 203 days in Haiti. Enforcing a simple contract takes 48 days in the Netherlands, but 1,459 days in Guatemala. A basic bankruptcy procedure takes less than a year in Singapore, but 10 years in India and Brazil. Burdensome procedures of this kind contribute to informality, reduce incentives to enter contracts with strangers, and discourage lending to firms.

### *Barriers to Competition*

Productivity improvements play a central role in growth processes. And competitive pressures drive firms to improve their productivity. Yet government policies often hinder rather than facilitate competition, whether through the erection of trade barriers, licensing regimes, or the sanctioning of monopolies or cartels. Though the beneficiary firms are unlikely to complain, the evidence shows that firms facing stronger competitive pressure are at least 50 percent more likely to introduce new products, upgrade existing products, or introduce new technologies.

## Four Underlying Challenges

If a good investment climate plays such a key role in growth and poverty reduction, and is now more widely understood to do so, why do such huge variations in investment climate conditions persist?

Part of the answer undoubtedly lies in the breadth of the agenda. Indeed, for this reason alone, thoroughgoing reforms may take decades or longer. But there are also four deeper challenges that can frustrate progress in rich and poor countries alike: rent seeking and corruption, credibility gaps, a lack of social consensus, and poor institutional fit.

### *Rent Seeking and Corruption*

Government policies shaping the investment climate are an enticing target for firms seeking special privileges and for politicians and officials seeking to benefit from the exchange. No country can claim to be immune from such pressures. But countries with less established checks on government behavior, including many developing countries, can be particularly handicapped by these problems, leading to deep distortions in investment climate policymaking. Firms benefiting from special privileges; officials benefiting from the income opportunities from onerous, ambiguous, and opaque regulations; and politicians benefiting from the ability to punish and reward particular groups have strong incentives to resist reform.

### *Building Credibility*

Firms and entrepreneurs do not make investment decisions on the basis of the formal content of laws and policy pronouncements alone, but rather on their expectations of whether those laws and policies will be implemented and sustained over time. The credibility of reforms is thus critical to their impact. Though this is true in all countries, many developing countries must deal with the legacy of past government behaviors and so take special efforts to convince firms of their commitment to reform.

### *Social Consensus and Legitimacy*

Broad public support plays an important role in enabling and sustaining reforms in this area. It may be necessary to overcome the resistance of those who benefit from the status quo. And it may be necessary to sustain the reforms in the face of short-term adjustment costs or more concerted opposition from disaffected groups. A high level of transparency and consultation in the design and implementation of reforms may reduce policy uncertainty and concerns about corruption or rent seeking. But it is also important to take account of the impact of reforms on disadvantaged groups in society and to be sensitive to distributional concerns more generally.

### *Ensuring a Good Institutional Fit*

Improving laws and policies requires more than the adoption of approaches copied from successful countries. To function effectively, laws and policies often require significant adaptation to the local environment, including factors such as administrative capacity and safeguards against the misuse of discretion. In the absence of sufficient adaptation, so-called reforms may have negligible or even perverse results. This has important implications for consultants from rich countries, who can have a tendency to recommend the adoption of laws and polices from their home country, regardless of where they are recommending them.

## Setting Priorities

It is always tempting for specialists to declare that their particular subject area should be the top priority for developing countries. From time to time, various fashions prevail in this as in other fields, whether the theme du jour is industrial clusters, public-private partnerships, or special schemes to facilitate access to finance. Alas, such universal recipes must confront some serious realities.

The first is that the main obstacles facing entrepreneurs can vary widely across countries. Indeed, surveys show that firms even in neighboring countries with many similar characteristics can perceive very different constraints, as a simple comparison of Bulgaria, Georgia, and Ukraine shows (figure 2-5). An aggregate indicator of investment climate quality would obscure such differences.

**Figure 2-5.** No Universal Priorities . . . Even in the Same Region

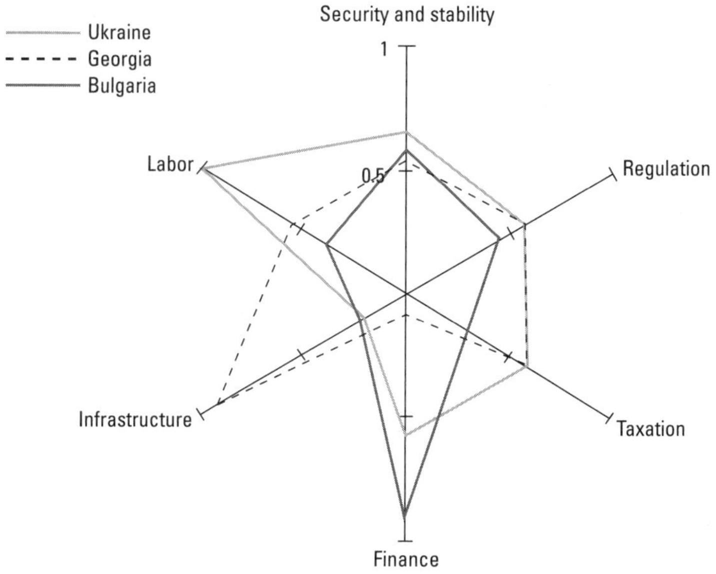

Source: World Bank survey data.

Second, the surveys show that there are often big variations in the constraints faced by firms in different locations within the one country. Thus, firms in cities in China and in states in India and Brazil report large variations in investment climate conditions, including the reliability of infrastructure or the burdens of regulatory compliance.

Third, the same investment conditions can affect firms even in identical locations very differently. Thus, the same investment climate may affect firms differently depending on whether they are engaged in exporting as opposed to serving the local market, or are capital or labor intensive. The survey data show that there are also some systematic differences between firms based on their size, with smaller firms generally facing the most severe constraints. Larger firms are typically better equipped to deal with distorted finance markets (due to sources of internal finance, assets to pledge as collateral, and established reputations), to cope with poor infrastructure through self-provision, and to cope with potential policy uncertainty through better access to politicians and officials. One implication is that efforts to improve the overall investment climate will tend to deliver disproportionate benefits to smaller firms. This is encouraging news, particularly given the poor track record of many schemes intended to confer special benefits on smaller firms.

Reflecting these considerations, there is no substitute for undertaking a thorough analysis in each environment to identify the most important constraints. An effective dialogue with firms themselves is an important part of this process, and that dialogue needs to extend beyond representatives of large and influential firms to include the perspectives of a broader range of actors.

## Where Does Finance Fit In?

A common challenge facing small entrepreneurs everywhere is access to finance to fund their ventures. Because they typically have limited credit histories and few assets to pledge as collateral, they are often seen as high-risk customers for banks. As a result, they tend to rely more heavily than larger firms on internal funds to finance their investments, and they also rely more on family and friends for external funding.

The situation facing small entrepreneurs in developing countries is often even more challenging, for several reasons:

—The banking sector is often not very competitive and in many cases is still dominated by state-owned banks pursuing political mandates and with weak credit appraisal skills. These banks often focus on meeting the financing needs of governments, and their regulations restrict interest rates.

—Entrepreneurs often lack formal title to land and other property that might otherwise be used as collateral.

—Weak contract enforcement mechanisms increase the risk of lending without collateral.

—In many cases there are no mechanisms to help entrepreneurs establish and demonstrate their creditworthiness.

Until recently, governments interested in helping smaller entrepreneurs focused on addressing the symptoms rather than the underlying causes. They instituted a range of special programs offering directed or subsidized credit or special loan guarantees. The track record of such interventions in developing countries has been dismal. Though more credit was indeed often provided, it typically went to connected firms, and the additional distortions to credit markets exacerbated the underlying difficulties.

Newer approaches focus on addressing the underlying problems. Banking sectors are being deregulated and privatized, and new-bank and nonbank financial intermediaries are entering the market to respond to underserved clients. Schemes to secure rights to land are being implemented, and registries for movable property are being established as well. Credit information bureaus are being established to help firms establish their credit records, and more countries are addressing issues related to the enforcement of smaller claims. Taken together, these approaches are expanding opportunities for smaller firms to access credit, without the costs and distortions of earlier approaches.

## A Process, Not an Event

The nature and breadth of the investment climate agenda mean that progress requires more than the one-off, "stroke-of-the-pen" privatization and trade reforms pursued in the early 1990s. Reforms in this area require ongoing attention to identify and address binding constraints. And the nature of those constraints will evolve over time as earlier constraints are relaxed and markets evolve. It is a process, not an event.

Successful reformers recognize this and create specialist institutions to support an ongoing process of reform. They create institutions to manage consultations with firms and other stakeholders. They establish mechanisms to systematically review existing constraints, and they often complement these with mechanisms to help ensure that new policy or regulatory proposals do not introduce unjustified burdens. Finally, they actively reach out to their communities to build a consensus for reform, including by ensuring that the benefits of reform are shared widely in society.

## Reference

World Bank. 2004. *World Development Report 2005: A Better Investment Climate for Everyone.* Oxford University Press. Contains sources for all data and supporting references mentioned in the text.

# 3

## *Leveraging the Development Impact of Business in the Fight against Global Poverty*

JANE NELSON

DURING THE PAST TWO DECADES, the forces of political transformation, economic globalization, and technical innovation have resulted in an unprecedented transfer of assets to the private sector, bringing private enterprise to the heart of the international development agenda. Though small and medium-size enterprises and microenterprises account for the bulk of economic activity and job creation in most countries, the global reach and influence of multinational corporations have grown substantially. The United Nations estimates that their number has almost doubled from 37,000 in 1990 to more than 60,000 today, with some 800,000 foreign affiliates and millions of suppliers and distributors operating along their global value chains (Nelson 2001).

Linked to these trends, private capital flows to developing countries have risen more than fivefold since 1990 and now outstrip official development assistance. Although most of these flows are targeted at a small number of key emerging markets and their effects are not always beneficial to recipient countries, there is a growing consensus that private sector investment and development—both domestic and foreign and both large scale and small—have a vital role to play in driving economic growth and helping to alleviate poverty.

Under the right conditions, private enterprises offer the potential to increase innovation, spur wealth creation, transfer technology, raise productivity,

**Jane Nelson** is a senior fellow and director of the Corporate Social Responsibility Initiative at the Kennedy School of Government, Harvard University, and a director at the Prince of Wales International Business Leaders Forum (IBLF). She is coauthor of the World Economic Forum's four Global Corporate Citizenship reports since 2002 and a member of its Global Governance Initiative working group.

"One of the key leadership challenges of our time is to find new ways to harness the innovation, technology, networks and problem-solving skills of the private sector, in partnership with others, to support international development goals. And to do so in a manner that makes sound business sense, and does not replace or undermine the role of government. Business leaders have a growing interest, both in terms of risk management and harnessing new opportunities, to get engaged."

—J. Nelson, D. Prescott, and S. Held, *Partnering for Success: Business Perspectives on Multi-Stakeholder Partnerships,* World Economic Forum, 2005.

meet basic needs, enhance living standards, and improve the quality of life for millions of people around the globe (see United Nations Commission on the Private Sector and Development 2004; World Bank 2004, 2005). Efficient markets and good governance, at both the global and national levels, are essential conditions for enabling the private sector to fulfill this potential. So too is profitable and responsible business leadership—leadership based on clear values and on a commitment to delivering or, at a minimum, protecting both market value *and* social value.

## What Does This Mean in Practice?

At its foundation, such business leadership requires the implementation of responsible business practices and standards in areas such as ethics, the environment, labor, and human rights—everywhere a company operates—to manage risks, minimize negative externalities and effects, and protect existing market and social value. It also involves the creation of innovative new business models, investment strategies, and partnerships aimed at harnessing the core competencies, resources, and problem-solving skills of private enterprise to create new market and social value. And it involves efforts by the private sector, working in partnership with others, to help establish the appropriate conditions, institutions, and enabling environment for good governance and private sector development.

None of this is easy. The challenges of ensuring efficient markets and good governance should not be underestimated. These challenges include overcoming "bad governance," such as corruption and the legacy of repressive regimes, failed states, and conflict, and improving "weak governance" resulting from inadequate public capacity and administrative and institutional capability to serve citizens' needs. They also require efforts to address "indifferent governance" or a lack of political will, in both donor and developing countries, when it comes to prioritizing and allocating resources to urgent development needs.

Nor should we underestimate the complex and at times contradictory set of pressures and expectations faced by today's business leaders. They are being called on to engage with activists as well as analysts, to manage social and environmental risks as well as market and political risks, to be accountable for their nonfinancial as well as their financial performance, and to cooperate as well as compete, often with nontraditional allies focused on unfamiliar issues, ranging from HIV/AIDS to climate change. They are under pressure from regulators, investors, consumers, trade unions, and nongovernmental organizations (NGOs) to deliver outstanding performance not only in terms of competitiveness, profitability, and market growth, but also in their corporate governance and corporate responsibility. Many of them face the unprecedented challenge of having to deliver shareholder value while also delivering, and demonstrating that they are delivering, societal value.

In part, these increased pressures and expectations are an understandable response to the corporate ethics and governance scandals of recent years. They also reflect public concerns about corporate complicity, both real and perceived, in a range of labor, human rights, and environmental problems. At the same time, these growing expectations of business reflect a belief that large companies, with their global influence, reach, and resources, offer some of the world's best hopes for helping to solve pressing development issues.

There is a danger in some cases that too much is being expected of business, especially in light of the competitive pressures and operational constraints faced by even the largest global corporations. It is crucial, therefore, to emphasize that even the most profitable, responsible, and innovative business practices can achieve little in tackling global poverty in the absence of good government, underpinned by political will and public interest.

Despite the challenges, a growing number of leadership examples give cause for hope. These range from innovative activities by individual firms to collective action by groups of companies to global multistakeholder alliances. Examples include:

1. *The development of new business models and innovative investment strategies at the level of individual firms.* Some of these are focused on creating jobs and livelihood opportunities for poor people, others on exploring economically viable approaches to addressing environmental challenges and delivering

goods and services to low-income consumers and communities, and some are helping to build public capacity and administrative capability. A few of the hundreds of examples that are emerging are outlined in box 3-1.

*2. The collective engagement of companies through sector-based, issue-focused, or national business coalitions.* Companies are working together, often with major competitors, to tackle social, environmental, and development challenges that no one company can address effectively on its own. They include national business leadership networks such as the Philippine Business for Social Progress, the Thai Business Initiative for Rural Development, South Africa's National Business Initiative, Tanzania's Private Sector Initiative, and Brazil's Instituto Ethos. Issue-focused alliances are also emerging, such as the Global Business Coalition against HIV/AIDS and the Business Alliance for Food Fortification, as are industry-wide initiatives, such as the chemical industry's Responsible Care initiative, the International Council for Metals and Mining, and the International Tourism Partnership.

*3. The establishment of cross-sector or multistakeholder alliances.* Companies are also partnering with governments and/or civil society organizations to jointly support efforts aimed at improving national and global governance systems, developing and spreading international norms and standards, shifting market frameworks, mobilizing resources, or increasing political support for development. Examples initiated or led by governmental agencies include the UN Global Compact, which brings together more than 3,000 companies with UN agencies, trade unions, and human rights and environmental NGOs; the United Nations Development Program's Growing Sustainable Business initiative; the U.S. Agency for International Development's Global Development Alliance; the World Bank's Development Marketplace; the Global Fund to Fight AIDS, Tuberculosis, and Malaria; and the Extractive Industries Transparency Initiative, to name just a few. Similar multistakeholder efforts led by private actors but with public sector partners include the Marine and Forest Stewardship Councils, the Global Alliance for Vaccines and Immunization, the Global Alliance for Improved Nutrition, the Global Road Safety Partnership, the Partnership for Quality Medical Donations, the Fair Labor Association, and the Equator Principles, which bring together some of the world's major providers of project finance.

In summary, there are a growing and wide-ranging number of examples of companies actively engaged in supporting international development goals. Such initiatives cannot, and should not, replace the role of government, but they can make a valuable contribution. The following section provides a conceptual framework for analyzing this contribution.

BOX 3-1

## Innovative New Business Models and Investment Strategies by Individual Firms

Some of these examples are hybrids of philanthropic models that harness core commercial competencies, skills, and products, while others are being established as profit-making ventures and business activities—but all are focused on improving the access of low-income households, entrepreneurs, and communities to essential products, services, resources, and opportunities.

*Spreading Access to Economic Opportunity*

In Ghana and Tanzania, Unilever is working with small-scale producers to source raw materials from indigenous plants, and enabling small-scale distributors to sell affordable products to low-income households in countries such as Brazil, India, and Indonesia. Starbucks is working with Conservation International and local farmers to support sustainable coffee production and more reliable incomes. SC Johnson is undertaking similar efforts with KickStart and small-scale growers of pyrethrum in Kenya. CEMEX is cooperating with Ashoka in Mexico to deliver low-income housing, job creation, and training. In Kazakhstan, Chevron and Citigroup are working with the United Nations and local partners to deliver small business services, as is BP in Azerbaijan. In the Middle East, where more than 60 percent of the population is under the age of twenty-five years, companies such as Abdul Latif Jameel and Shell are supporting youth enterprise initiatives.

*Providing Access to Pro-Poor Financial Services*

Citigroup, Deutsche Bank, Credit Suisse, Barclays, ABN AMRO, Calvert, ANZ, Standard Bank, and Merrill Lynch are among leading financial institutions that have started to develop financial services for poor people, ranging from microcredit to insurance, saving, and investment products.

*Improving Access to Information Technology*

Efforts to harness information and communications technology to support education, enterprise development, and humanitarian relief in developing countries are being undertaken by Cisco Systems, Microsoft, Vodafone, IBM, HP, Ericsson, Dell, Ayala, and Infosys, among others.

*Ensuring Access to Clean and Affordable Water and Energy*

Shell is working with the United Nations and others in Uganda to catalyze the pro-poor market for solar home systems, aimed at both increasing access to energy and tackling indoor pollution and health problems. BP is doing likewise in the Philippines, EDF is supporting off-grid energy access in Madagascar, and ABB is working with the WWF on sustainable energy access in Tanzania. Companies such as Thames Water/RWE, Suez, General Electric, and Coca-Cola are exploring new financing mechanisms and technologies to improve access to clean water and sanitation.

*Increasing Access to Health and Safety*

Most major pharmaceutical companies are now engaged in efforts to improve access to essential medicines through a variety of research and development initiatives, preferential pricing, and product donation programs. Some are also investing money and management expertise in efforts to improve public health system capacity more broadly, such as Abbott Laboratories in Tanzania; Merck in Botswana; Pfizer in Uganda; and BMS, J&J, and GSK elsewhere in Africa. Companies with large developing country work forces, such as Coca-Cola, Anglo-American, Chevron, Rio Tinto, Unilever, and ExxonMobil, are also developing new approaches to support employees and local communities in the fight against infectious diseases. Companies such as GM, 3M, InBev, Diageo, and SABMiller are working to improve road safety. Major food companies are engaging in food fortification efforts. And retail companies such as Nike, Reebok, the Gap, and Pentland have led efforts to improve working conditions, health, and safety in contractors' factories.

For more information, see Nelson (1996, 2001, 2006); World Business Council for Sustainable Development (2004, 2005); Prahalad (2005); Hart (2005); and Shell Foundation (2005).

"Private firms are at the heart of the development process. Driven by the quest for profits, firms of all types—from farmers and microentrepreneurs to local manufacturing companies and multinational enterprises—invest in new ideas and new facilities that strengthen the foundation of economic growth and prosperity. They provide more than 90 percent of jobs—creating opportunities for people to apply their talents and improve their situations. They provide the goods and services needed to sustain life and improve living standards. They are also the main source of tax revenues, contributing to public funding for health, education, and other services. Firms are thus central actors in the quest for growth and poverty reduction."

—*World Development Report 2005*, World Bank, 2004

## The Potential Contribution of Business to Development

There is wide variation in the specific contributions that different companies can make to protecting and creating social and market value and to supporting key development goals such as poverty alleviation. Their contribution depends not only on the type of development intervention needed—such as increasing access to jobs, income, education, health, energy, water, technology, and markets; or improving governance and public capacity—but also on factors such as the industry sector and the company's business model, ownership structure, and size. While recognizing the crucial development role of small enterprises, medium-size firms, and microenterprises, this chapter focuses primarily on the contribution of large companies, both multinationals and large national companies.

The effectiveness and scope of the corporate contribution to development and poverty alleviation also depends on location. This refers not only to the situational impact of different countries, cultures, political systems, and circumstances but also to whether the activity is being carried out by corporate headquarters operating at a global or national level or by a local business partner, subsidiary, or operating unit of the company.

The scale and sustainability of the development contribution also depends on the number of companies involved. As outlined in the previous section, this can vary from a company acting in its individual capacity—either within its own business operations and supply chain or through its own philanthropic foundation or community investment programs—to companies operating on a collective basis with each other and to more complex multistakeholder alliances that bring together groups of companies with government bodies and NGOs.

Despite these differences, almost all companies regardless of industry sector and other variables have the potential to make a contribution to development and poverty alleviation through the following three spheres of business impact and influence (this framework is adapted from Nelson 1996; see also Nelson and Prescott 2003; Nelson 2003):

1. *Core business operations and investments*—including the company's activities and relationships in the workplace, in the marketplace, and along the supply chain. The greatest and most sustainable contribution that any company can make to development is through carrying out its core business activities in a profitable, productive, and responsible manner. The key goals should be to minimize any negative effects on development and poverty alleviation that may arise from these activities and to increase and leverage positive effects.

2. *Strategic philanthropy and community investment*—aimed at mobilizing not only money but also the company's people, products, and premises to help support and strengthen local communities and nonprofit partners.

3. *Public policy dialogue, advocacy, and institution building*—efforts by companies, either individually or collectively, to participate in relevant public policy dialogues and advocacy platforms with both developing country governments and donor governments, and to help governments build public capacity and strengthen institutions to better serve their citizens.

These three spheres of business impact and influence can also be envisaged as a company's "development footprint"—the extent of which will vary depending on the company, industry sector, and situation in question.

One of the most interesting developments in recent years has been the emergence of what can be described as "hybrid approaches." These are essentially business models, practices, or partnerships that combine the company's core competencies and commercial acumen with social investment, philanthropy, and public finance (World Economic Forum 2005). Such approaches are being used to support projects that may not currently meet commercial hurdle rates but that have the potential to become commercially viable over the longer term, while explicitly addressing a development or social need.

Linked to these hybrid approaches, the term "blended value investing" has been coined to describe private investment strategies and instruments that explicitly include social and/or environmental factors into investment decisions.[1] In their 2005 report *Private Investment for Social Goals: Building the Blended Value Capital Market*, the World Economic Forum, International Finance Corporation, and Rockefeller Foundation comment, "Financial returns in blended value investments may be at risk-adjusted market rates or below-market rates. These types of investments inhabit a space between philanthropy, where no financial return is expected, and pure financial investments, where social considerations are not a factor and financial profit is maximized" (World Economic Forum, International Finance Corporation, and Rockefeller Foundation 2005).

It is important to emphasize that in each of the three spheres of corporate impact and influence, a company's contribution to poverty alleviation may be negative or positive, depending on how the company actually carries out its activities and with whom it engages. The following section outlines six key strategies that most companies can employ to minimize the negative and leverage the positive effects of their activities and to strengthen their overall impact on development, while also protecting market value or creating new value for the company and its owners.

## Corporate Strategies to Strengthen the Development Impact of Business

Companies have six key strategies that they can implement to protect existing market and societal value and to create new value as follows (adapted from Jackson and Nelson 2004):

*1. Compliance.* In addition to ensuring compliance with national laws, a growing number of companies are also cooperating with voluntary international or sector-specific principles, norms, and standards. These range from purely voluntary, unmonitored frameworks to more rigorous systems that call for peer reviews, external audits, certification, and public reporting. Though legal compliance should be seen as a minimum requirement for strengthening the business contribution to development, even this basic strategy is beset by operational and governance challenges for companies with hundreds of operating units and business partners in numerous different countries and legal jurisdictions. Ensuring that the company has policies and systems in

1. Jed Emerson, Timothy Freundlich, and Shari Berenbach, *The Investor's Toolkit,* 2004 (www.blendedvalue.org/publications/additional.html).

place to address this challenge—including board-level oversight—is an important demonstration of good intent.

*2. Control of risks, liabilities, costs, and negative effects.* Going beyond compliance, companies can also implement systems to ensure that they identify, manage, and where necessary ameliorate ethical, social, and environmental risks, in addition to more familiar market, financial, operational, and political risks. Recent research by the Kennedy School's Corporate Social Responsibility Initiative, Booz Allen Hamilton, and others illustrates the growing value of stakeholder engagement as an effective strategy for this broader approach to risk management (Kytle and Ruggie 2005).

*3. Charity and community investment.* Moving from value protection to value creation, companies can create social value, while either protecting or enhancing their own market value, through effective philanthropy or community investment strategies. These are most likely to have a positive impact on both social *and* market value when they are aligned with not only community needs but also corporate competencies and interests—for example, energy companies supporting projects to improve access to energy, logistics companies providing distribution support for humanitarian crises, ICT companies helping to improve access to technology, and health care companies providing medical donations.

*4. Creating new social and market value.* The most strategic approach for strengthening the company's contribution to development comes through innovation in new products, services, processes, investment mechanisms, and even business models that directly align development needs with profit-making business opportunities. As outlined in the previous section, some of these opportunities may offer the company a full market-driven financial return, while others may require a combination of commercial and social or public financing, at least at the outset, to make them a viable proposition (figure 3-1).

Moving beyond the level of individual firm strategies and management frameworks, some development challenges directly affect a company's profitability or operating environment, which it is unable to address effectively, legitimately, or to a sufficient scale on its own. Examples could include tackling bribery and corruption beyond the company's own business operations, improving the enabling environment for private investment, supporting education reform, strengthening public capacity and institutions, shifting markets toward more socially or environmentally sustainable paradigms, and ensuring industry-wide ethical, social, or environmental standards to avoid

**Figure 3-1.** Strategies to Strengthen the Contribution to Development at the Level of the Individual Firm

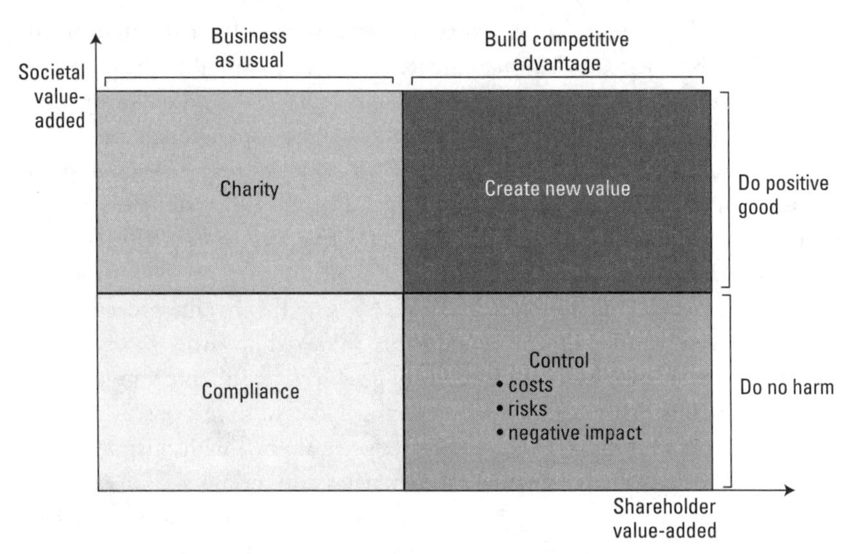


Source: Adapted from Jackson and Nelson (2004).

"free-rider" problems. In such cases, there are two key strategic options for companies aiming to strengthen their contribution to development:

*5. Collective corporate action.* Companies can address certain development challenges by engaging in collective corporate action. This can often be achieved through representative business organizations, such as chambers of commerce, organizations of employers, or trade and industry groups. It can also be achieved through more targeted business leadership groups as outlined in the first section of this chapter, for example, with a specific social and environmental mandate such as national business councils for sustainable development or national business coalitions to tackle HIV/AIDS.

*6. Cross-sector engagement and multistakeholder partnerships.* A final strategy, with relevance at the global, national, or local level, is for companies to participate in formal alliances with key development actors in other sectors—government bodies, donor agencies, NGOs, trade unions, universities, and the like. Such alliances vary widely in the formality and rigor of their governance and operational structures as well as in their focus and purpose. They can be structured as consultation mechanisms or as operational and delivery mechanisms. They can help to protect market and social value—as is the case for alliances to set standards and improve public and private governance systems. They can also help to create new market and social value—as is the case for alliances to mobilize financial and other resources from different sectors to develop new models that support key development objectives.

The "added value" of collective corporate action and cross-sector or multi-stakeholder partnerships comes from their ability to confer greater legitimacy and/or enable greater leverage of resources than any one of the participants could achieve on its own. But they are not a panacea. Research by the World Bank, United Nations, International Business Leaders Forum, AccountAbility, and others shows that these alliances can have high transaction and operational costs. They may also face substantial governance and accountability challenges. Despite these challenges, they can be a useful addition to a diversified portfolio of strategies used by companies and other development actors to strengthen the development impact of business.

## Recommendations

The previous section reviewed strategies that companies can take individually, collectively, and in partnership with other sectors to strengthen their own development impact. Clearly, governments and other stakeholders—such as investors, customers, employees, trade unions, and NGOs—can also influence the behavior and strategies of business in ways that strengthen the private sector's role in development and poverty alleviation.

The following recommendations suggest eight areas of action for business leaders and some of their most influential stakeholders to consider on either an individual or collective basis.

*1. Define a corporate strategy for supporting development goals.* On an individual basis, companies can identify and set targets for addressing key development challenges that either represent a particular risk or opportunity to their business and/or can be addressed through the application of their core competencies, skills, and resources. They can report on progress in their annual report and other communications tools, engage employees, and raise awareness of board members and key stakeholders, including institutional investors, to increase understanding and support for the "business case" of engaging in these development issues.

*2. Co-invest with development agencies.* There are a growing number of initiatives by development agencies to create formal partnerships with the private sector. These include the U.S. Agency for International Development's Global Development Alliance, the United Nations Development Program's

Growing Sustainable Business initiative, the Global Fund's co-investment framework, and the International Finance Corporation's Corporate Citizenship Facility, to name just a few. Large companies should explore opportunities to "co-invest" with these agencies and with NGOs in innovative development initiatives that make sound business sense. Supporting local economic empowerment through enterprise development, training, technology transfer, improved access to credit, and youth enterprise as well as human capital development through providing access to better health and education are key areas where co-investment can make a vital contribution. Another key focus for co-investment could be on efforts to strengthen the capacity of business leadership groups in developing countries and to build public capacity and strengthen public institutions.

*3. Offer "blended value" investment options in employee pension funds.* Companies can offer employees socially responsible investment (SRI) options in their corporate pension schemes. There are clearly a number of fiduciary issues that need to be addressed here, but there is great potential for corporate pension funds, foundations, and SRI investors to explore these issues together. Such coalitions can also advocate for development agencies—such as the United Nations and World Bank, development NGOs, trade unions, and foundations—to do likewise with their own investment portfolios.

*4. Explore innovative fiscal incentives.* Governments, business groups, and development agencies can work together to develop fiscal incentives to encourage increased investment and/or philanthropic giving to developing countries or to specific development issues. Fiscal instruments can also be employed to discourage socially and environmentally irresponsible behavior and externalities.

*5. Develop procurement and financing requirements.* Companies that source from, distribute through, or finance other companies can influence the behavior of these companies through their supply chain management and financing policies. Likewise, governments, development banks, export guarantee agencies, and development agencies can influence corporate behavior through their own requirements and guidelines for procurement and the provision of public finance and government support. Effective examples already exist in all these areas and could be emulated or scaled up.

*6. Support international norms, principles, and standards.* There are a number of credible voluntary mechanisms with which companies can cooperate that provide guidelines, frameworks, or certification systems for responsible corporate behavior in developing countries. The majority of companies have yet to engage with such mechanisms.

*7. Host project visits.* One of the best ways to engage decisionmakers is for them to visit innovative development projects on the ground. For example, add a project visit to board meetings held in developing countries or require board members to visit company operations in a developing country. Add project visits to trade missions or participate in tailored programs such as the International Business Leaders Forum's "Crossing Borders" initiative and the ImagineNations Group's "Seeing Is Believing" program. Encourage high-potential young managers to visit and/or volunteer on development projects.

*8. Integrate international development issues into education.* Companies, development agencies, and academic institutions could do much more to ensure better coverage of development issues in relevant school and university curricula. At Harvard's 2005 commencement, former president Lawrence Summers addressed what he described as "perhaps the defining development of our time . . . the growing integration between the developing world and the developed world, and the rising importance of the developing world in shaping human history." Today's leaders need to do a better job of educating tomorrow's leaders about the risks and opportunities of this process. At a minimum, such issues should become an integral component in a company's own internal leadership training and executive development programs. Companies can also support campaigns to better educate the general public on critical global challenges.

These are just a few of the actions that major companies and their stakeholders can take, and some are already taking, to strengthen the business contribution to international development. The subject is likely to grow in importance, both as a risk and as an opportunity for business. Leaders in all sectors ignore it at their peril.

## References

Hart, S. 2005. *Capitalism at the Crossroads: The Unlimited Business Opportunities in Solving the World's Most Difficult Problems.* Philadelphia: Wharton School Publishing.

Jackson, Ira, and Jane Nelson. 2004. *Profits with Principles: Seven Strategies for Delivering Value with Values.* New York: Random House.

Kytle, B., and J. Ruggie. 2005. *Corporate Social Responsibility as Risk Management.* Working Paper 1, Corporate Social Responsibility Initiative. Cambridge, Mass.: John F. Kennedy School of Government, Harvard University.

Nelson, Jane. 1996. *Business as Partners in Development: Building Wealth for Countries, Companies, and Communities.* Washington, D.C.: World Bank, United Nations Development Program, and International Business Leaders Forum.

———. 2001. *Building Partnerships: Cooperation between the United Nations and the Private Sector.* New York: United Nations Department for Public Information.

———. 2003. *Economic Multipliers: Revisiting the Core Responsibility and Contribution of Business to Development.* London: International Business Leaders Forum.

———. 2006. *Building Linkages for Competitive and Responsible Entrepreneurship: Innovative Partnerships to Foster Small Enterprise to Promote Economic Growth and Reduce Poverty in Developing Countries.* Vienna and Cambridge, Mass.: United Nations Industrial Development Organization and John F. Kennedy School of Government, Harvard University.

Nelson, J., and D. Prescott. 2003. *Business and the Millennium Development Goals: A Framework for Action.* New York: United Nations Development Program and International Business Leaders Forum.

Nelson, J., D. Prescott, and S. Held. 2005. *Partnering for Success: Business Perspectives on Multi-Stakeholder Partnerships.* Geneva: World Economic Forum, in collaboration with International Business Leaders Forum and John F. Kennedy School of Government, Harvard University.

Prahalad, C. K. 2005. *The Fortune at the Bottom of the Pyramid: Eradicating Poverty through Profits.* Philadelphia: Wharton School Publishing.

Shell Foundation. 2005. *Enterprise Solutions to Poverty: Opportunities and Challenges for the International Development Community and Big Business.* London.

United Nations Commission on the Private Sector and Development. 2004. *Unleashing Entrepreneurship: Making Business Work for the Poor.* New York.

World Bank. 2004. *World Development Report 2005: A Better Investment Climate for Everyone.* Oxford University Press.

———. 2005. *Doing Business in 2006: Creating Jobs.* Washington, D.C.

World Business Council for Sustainable Development. 2004. *Doing Business with the Poor: A Field Guide.* Geneva.

———. 2005. *Business for Development: Business Solutions in Support of the Millennium Development Goals.* Geneva.

World Economic Forum. 2005. *Global Governance Initiative, 2005 Annual Report.* Geneva.

World Economic Forum, International Finance Corporation, and Rockefeller Foundation. 2005. *Private Investment for Social Goals: Building the Blended Value Capital Market.* Geneva, Washington, and New York.

# 4

## *Blended Value Investment and a Living Return*

TIMOTHY FREUNDLICH

CONVENTIONAL INVESTING, and the subsequent creation of economic value, has by and large been viewed as an activity separate and distinct from efforts to create social value and positive environmental impact. The traditional view is that companies and investment managers fulfill their social responsibilities simply by generating the greatest possible financial return, regardless of the social and environmental costs involved, with each investor then deciding how best to "do good" with the profits. Essentially, the mainstream model says, "Let's maximize the risk-adjusted financial return in a vacuum, and then give it away later."

Today's investors face a challenge and an opportunity. By changing how we think about value within an investment frame, we can adopt the concept of "blended value" to utilize all available resources to promote environmental, social, and financial equitability and sustainability. By changing how we define our appetite for returns and shifting toward the concept of a "living return" (the conceptual sister to a "living wage"), we can begin to rebalance wealth in the world with consideration for how much is enough.

Timothy Freundlich is the director of strategic development for the Calvert Social Investment Foundation. This chapter borrows from certain sections and concepts of *The Investor's Toolkit,* by Jed Emerson, this author, and Shari Berenbach (2004) and other works in progress by the author and Emerson. Readers may download writings on the blended value proposition by Emerson (to whom great credit must be given for this concept) at www.blendedvalue.org. Research and editorial support for this chapter was provided by Loren Berlin.

Unequal wealth and income disparity have created a global "barbell," in which the middle class is a thin band between two extremes. On the right end of the barbell is the "wealthy weight" of the world's richest people, the 500 individuals with a collective income of $91 billion (the data here are from the United Nations Development Program). On the left end of the barbell is the "impoverished weight" of the world's poorest people, the almost 400 million people with a similar collective income of $91 billion. The weights are equal in size by dollar amount but radically disparate by the number of people.

Clearly, this polarization is not sustainable. Therefore, we must seek ways to flatten the wealth gap and build a more resilient social contract. It is in the industrial world owners' enlightened self-interest to realign the practice of investment, to promote a more equitable environmental-social-economic system. This brings us to blended value investment—an effort to realign the risk-reward paradigm and investor focus—to reflect and reinforce a sustainable world.

## What Is Blended Value Investment?

Traditionally, the social and environmental effects of investment decisions have been considered externalities, superfluous to the investment equation. There are two explanations for this misconception.

First, society tends to discount the ways in which values affect investment decisions. That is to say, people often believe investing is merely the act of putting one's dollars into a financial instrument. However, investing is fundamentally based on the individual's pursuit of personal goals and very basic human needs. We seek to create wealth in order to have choices regarding how we live our lives, provide for our families, and pursue our dreams. We seek to create wealth to build thriving economic systems to ensure that we live in safe and bountiful communities that allow us, and others, to achieve our greatest potential. Truly, the goal of creating economic wealth is seldom pursued in the abstract. Instead, it is a means to an end.

Second, investors can usually ignore the true costs of doing business, because social and environmental capital is not included in standard accounting practices. The social and environmental costs of doing business are pushed off corporations' financial statements. However, just because we do not consider the true implications of our investments does not mean that they do not exist. When we invest, we participate in a complex system of value creation that generates multiple returns with financial, social, and environmental implications. If we are to support a sustainable world, we must restructure our thinking to account for the true costs in natural resources and for society.

The starting point of the blended value investment proposition is the idea that realigning value (and values) is maximized when investors leverage their full assets in pursuit of their goals. This challenge of fully utilizing assets is perhaps starkest for charitable foundations in managing their assets. The traditional practice is to use 5 percent of the foundation's asset base to make grants each year, while 95 percent of its assets are managed with little or no consideration of its overall institutional goals. In other words, 5 percent of the foundation's assets are driving 100 percent of its institutional mission, while 95 percent of the investors' assets are, at best, neutral with regard to supporting the foundation's overall goals. Often, these investments are actually invested in companies that engage in practices that directly contradict the institution's mission (see Emerson 2002).

Such an investment strategy is akin to a baseball team manager choosing to send just two of his three dozen players through the rigors of spring training, regular practices, and coaching. The rest of the team members would be enrolled in "antitraining," in which they would be encouraged to park on the clubhouse couch all day, watch television reruns, and then go drinking at a local pub until the early hours of the morning. You can imagine how disastrous the team's performance, as a whole, would look on the field—even if the two preferred players consistently hit homeruns.

It is hard to argue that leaving such a huge portion of one's assets in antitraining mode maximizes the ability to attain investor goals. Whether for foundations to fulfill the fiduciary responsibility of their charitable charter, or for all investors who wish to align the entirety of their assets with their societal goals, the point is to send the whole team to training camp and then play the best game possible.

A blended value investment strategy seeks to identify an investor's full array of available assets—both financial and nonfinancial. For example, this may be conceptualized in terms of human capital as Time, Acumen, and Network capital, while financial capital can be broken down into Grants, Loans, and Equity. Thus, as an acronym, this spectrum of assets becomes a "TANGLE" of capital resources. (Readers should also see www.blendedvalue.org for a discussion of the 21st Century Foundation, which presents a unified investment strategy for foundations that calls for the full use of assets under management.) This investment strategy then assertively deploys these assets in support of the individual or institution's mission, thereby achieving the financial, social, and environmental goals the investor seeks to achieve.

A growing number of investors are executing strategies that intentionally seek to blend value. Consider the United States–based socially responsible investment landscape, for example. Strategies consist of issue screening, shareholder proxy voting, and community development investments. The market share has grown—from $40 billion in 1984 to $2.3 trillion in 2003, reaching 12 percent of all investment assets—as pension funds, institutional investors, and others have taken a more active stance toward shareholder involvement or introduced one or more social screens into their investment selection process. And U.S. investment in community development and microfinance has increased to $14 billion, at a recent compound annual growth rate of 36 percent, while private equity venture funds that seek social and environmental value are estimated at $2 billion (Social Investment Forum 2003; the private equity figure comes from RISE 2002).

Conceptually, financial assets may be divided into three general categories. The first includes capital that generates a blend of social and financial return, delivering a conventional market-rate risk-adjusted financial return. Assets either are neutral relative to the goals of the investor (for example, screening out industries or enterprises deemed to be in opposition to overall investor goals) or may be more proactively positioned to align with an investor's goals (for example, an investment creating jobs in a specific region).

The second category includes capital that generates a blend of social and financial return but delivers financial returns that are lower than the conventional risk-adjusted market rate in exchange for greater social returns. Assets are proactively reaching a high-value proposition in line with investors' goals but trade off a certain and measurable financial risk-reward concession (for example, a loan to an affordable housing development at less than going rates).

The third category includes capital that generates a core-mission-aligned social return but no financial return to the investor (other than, arguably, the tax deduction value at the front end, if such a deduction exists). The most common form of this type is a grant.

(In *The Investor's Toolkit*, we found utility in this three-category framework, but it still is worth observing that a quasi continuum exists, with the line between one or the other category blurred as the instruments available in the emerging social capital market become increasingly numerous and complex.)

If investors aim to fight global poverty, then what should they target, and how should they think about financial assets as tools to this end?

## Doing Well (Enough) While Doing Good

The first category of market-rate strategies seeks to exclude socially and environmentally "value-subtracting" enterprises, such as egregious polluters and corporations that employ child or forced labor. These strategies attempt to stop driving capital to enterprises that detract from a given investor's broader intent. Therefore, blended value thinking has necessary implications for altering the flows of capital. If most—if not all—capital flowed away from these enterprises, while investors simultaneously exercised shareholder power to change corporate behavior, and furthermore moved capital toward beneficial corporations, a natural global correction would occur.

A good example is the antiapartheid divestment movement in South Africa. More recent examples include:

—Cintas, a global garment manufacturer, which had been known for employing vendors that use sweatshop labor, recently agreed to adopt a code of conduct that all its vendors must also adopt, promising to pay vendor employees the minimum wage or industry wages (whichever is greater), provide safe and healthy work environments, refuse to use forced or prison labor, and refuse to use child labor. Cintas acted in response to negative publicity and pressure from an assortment of shareholder and labor groups. (The source for this description is www.cintas-corp.com.)

—Home Depot agreed to phase out the sale of wood from environmentally sensitive origins, including primary tropical forest and old-growth stands, due to pressure from a consortium of shareholder and environmental groups. (The source for this is www.foe.org.)

—ING, the eleventh-largest financial institution in the world, agreed to stop financing and directly investing in companies that produce controversial weapons, including land mines, cluster bombs, nuclear weapons, and uranium weapons. This was in response to the "My Money: Clear Conscience?" campaign launched in Belgium. (The source for this is www.netwerk-vlaanderen.be.)

—Most recently, in June 2005, the World Resources Institute and Merrill Lynch broke new ground by issuing stock recommendations that include climate change impact assessments—as seen in their report *Energy Security and Climate Change: Investing in the Clean Car Revolution* (World Resources Institute and Merrill Lynch 2005). This may herald a new trend of proactive, opportunistic, and broadly driven change in mainstream investor behavior. (The source for this is www.socialfunds.com/news/article.cgi/1741.html.)

Again, these activities are examples of blended value strategies for traditional investment that exclude enterprises with negative social value, exercise shareholder power to promote positive corporate behavior, and proactively allocate capital to firms that build positive outcomes in society. Though somewhat radical in their corrective activism, they do not require a fundamental blurring of conventional financial risk and return. Instead, they add social and environmental consideration to the equation, without demonstrable cost to the investor. (For example, the Domini Social Index's ten-year annualized return is 10.87 percent versus 10.18 percent for its benchmark, the Standard & Poor's 500, for the period ended May 31, 2005. Similarly, a study of socially responsible investment funds in the United States found that a higher percentage of these funds wind up in the top two quintiles, performing better than their conventional counterparts. The sources for these data are www.socialinvest.org and www.socialfunds.com.)

Perhaps more radical, the second category of assets is comprised of investments that offer lower than conventional market-rate financial returns in exchange for greater social value. Examples include equity and debt placements or loan guarantees in microfinance, cooperatives, and community development enterprises. They may reach a broad spectrum of activity, both in sectors and geography. (It is important to note that subtleties can delineate this category. It may be a question of instruments delivering a lower rate of return than comparables or carrying a longer time horizon or a greater degree of risk. Longer-term time horizons may allow an organization an extended period to create mission-based impact, higher risk may be expressed as subordination of the investment to leverage other senior capital or noncompensated country risk, and lower return may be required due to hybrid business models' ability to service debt.)

In market terms, these investments ask more fundamentally challenging questions of investors, such as:

—How do we really define value and return?

—Can we cross the conventional lines that force either return maximization or philanthropy?

—How much financial return is enough?

Admittedly, it will take more time for a consensus to emerge on the answers. But there is no doubt that investment in education, health, affordable housing, enterprise development, and independent media is a fundamental ingredient of positive social change. Already, path-breaking initiatives are rewriting the conventional rules of risk and return. Here are five examples:

—The Associação Nacional de Cooperação Agrícola (ANCA) is a Brazilian cooperative nonprofit organization that represents the settlements connected with the Movimento Sem Terra (Landless Workers Movement). ANCA provides educational opportunities to school-age children, as well as adults and community activists, by producing publications for the training and education of leaders in various worker movements. Approximately 7,000 books are sold each month, and that number continues to grow. ANCA has taken soft debt from a range of investors to provide working capital and financing to its members.

—Voxiva is a for-profit voice and data solutions provider that has developed new ways to use technology to address some of global health's most pressing challenges. From disease surveillance to adverse event reporting, Voxiva's applications allow public health agencies from Peru to Iraq to collect critical data from, and communicate with, frontline health workers in real time, empowering them to respond immediately. Investors have placed "patient" equity into this social venture to grow the budding enterprise.

—The Federation of Appalachian Housing Enterprises (FAHE) is an association of thirty nonprofit housing organizations producing affordable housing for low-income families across Appalachia, one of the most impoverished regions of the United States. FAHE clients have a median family income of $12,110. Cumulatively, FAHE groups have constructed or preserved almost 40,000 affordable homes. As a nonprofit, FAHE has been able to put to use millions of dollars in soft debt from investors to finance its housing activity.

—MicroVest is a debt and equity fund that invests in leading microfinance institutions throughout the developing world. It has raised limited partnership equity units to form a core of capital, to which it adds leveraged debt raised from individuals and institutions throughout the ten years of the limited partnership. It blends debt and equity, private partnership, and nonprofit structures.

—The Media Development Loan Fund (MDLF) is a nonprofit organization dedicated to assisting independent news outlets in emerging democracies to develop into financially sustainable media companies. MDLF invests in a range of debt and equity placements to television and radio broadcasters, newspapers, magazines, news agencies, and online media across Eastern Europe, the former Yugoslavia, the former Soviet Union, Asia, Africa, and Latin America. As such, MDLF is a revolving fund that takes soft debt from a range of investors.

These investments vary considerably—direct and intermediary, nonprofit and for profit, debt and equity. Yet all are examples of the rich landscape of activity that investors use to blend social and economic returns while reimagining the conventional risk-return paradigm. In so doing, investors create blended value both at the ground level and for the investor.

(These five examples barely scratch the surface of the wide spectrum of activity available. They come from a subsection of the Calvert Foundation's Community Investment Note portfolio experience, which is itself a global, pooled, fixed-income product used by retail and institutional investors. These groups are generally taking financing at longer terms and relatively low yield. More information is available at the Community Investment Profiles database, www.calvertfoundation.org/individual/research/profiles.html. The five examples given here are illustrations and are not meant as investment recommendations.)

## The Impact of Investment on Global Poverty

Imagine the impact of each $1 billion invested in a global, diversified portfolio of microfinance, affordable housing, cooperatives, and social enterprises. Roughly 1,140,000 jobs could be created, 160,000 affordable homes built or rehabilitated, and 70,000 cooperatives and nonprofit facilities financed each and every year. And these are just the primary effects. Each job, enterprise, or home has many ripple effects that create secondary but equally deep benefits over time. For example, microcredit increases household net worth, women's asset holdings, contraceptive use, and children's school attendance (Khandker and Pitt 2002).

(The statistics given in the last paragraph, which are based upon the Calvert Foundation's global social returns metrics collected from its portfolio organizations, are offered only to make a general point, not to stand up to academic testing. The Calvert Foundation administers portfolios that currently invest more than $100 million in 200 microfinance, community development, housing, and social enterprises, active in 60 countries. Weightings were—relatively arbitrarily—set at 68 percent microfinance, 20 percent affordable housing, and 12 percent cooperatives and nonprofit enterprises or facilities operating outside the United States.)

A total of $100 billion in private capital invested for a ten-year term could finance 1.14 billion microenterprise jobs, 160 million affordable housing units, and 70 million cooperatives or nonprofit facilities. At little more than one-half of 1 percent of the roughly $19.2 trillion in investment assets in the U.S. capital markets, this $100 billion would hardly be missed (Nelson Publications 2003; this chapter uses the U.S. markets, but certainly the percentage would be only a portion of the total industrial-world capital markets). This impact could become part of a full-spectrum industrial-world commitment to ending global poverty—the investment compliment to the UN's Millennium Development Goals (see www.un.org/millenniumgoals). Like the 191 UN member countries that have vowed to work together to achieve these goals, the world's investors could unify as a community to assist the world's poor.

Nor would the above commitment result in a variance of more than a few basis points of financial return on an annual basis. If these portfolios were to yield a net 3 percent (this would be a reasonable return based upon the Calvert Foundation's experience, net of management expenses and losses over time), versus a conventional market return of 8.85 percent (using a benchmark comprised of 60 percent Standard & Poor's 500 and 40 percent Lehman Aggregate Bond Index returns for the ten-year period ended May 31, 2005), the impact would be 3/100ths of 1 percent (3 basis points) a year—a small price to pay by any standard.

## Moving Blended Value Investment to the Bottom of the Pyramid

Do the global microfinance, social enterprise, and community development markets have the capacity to deploy $100 billion in debt and equity investment? Could investors even find the groups in which to invest? Perhaps not tomorrow, but capacity is growing quickly. As myriad microfinance and community development organizations all over the world scale up, the amount of capital they can and must employ will radically expand. Of note, microfinance institutions today reach only $4 billion of the estimated $300 billion demand for providing affordable financial services to the bottom of the pyramid.

(There is little doubt that the broad landscape of development organizations will need significant new capital, assuming the market continues to grow at historic rates. One recent analysis of just the Calvert Foundation's core portfolio indicated that an additional $5 billion would be required over the next few years to adequately capitalize them. The microfinance projection for this is from Grameen Foundation USA 2005.)

Would the capital market infrastructure require a significant "donor investment" in capacity building? Certainly, up-front outlays would be necessary, as would more efficient capital markets and a larger set of intermediaries. But the point here is that once the supply and demand emerge, the implementation tactics and infrastructure will follow.

So, what would it take to actually move this amount of capital from investors to far-flung enterprises? It is true that managing many relationships between investors and investees is intensely inefficient and prohibitively costly. Investors often lack a meaningful analysis of community development, microfinance, and social enterprises at the local level, while enterprises are interested in identifying capital as efficiently as possible but do not know where to go.

In the case of this early-stage market, the interests of both suppliers and users of capital will best be served by market intermediaries and a new generation of financial instruments that yield a blended financial and social return. We will need to rely upon aggregators, administrators, and consultants to move funds on an increasingly large and efficient scale. Though there are emerging funds, managers, and analysts, the number of intermediaries making up the market infrastructure is limited. It will be necessary to significantly augment the blended value capital markets to enhance their ability to handle greater flows of funds.

Finally, in addition to the amount of both time and expense related to working in this fragmented environment, the terms and conditions of capital are often out of alignment with effective strategies for creating social impact in various sectors. There will need to be both new developments of "equity-like" debt for nonprofits and an increased appetite in the markets for placing "patient" equity into social venture for-profits.

## Investing in Tomorrow's Global Contract

The social and environmental contract is stretched to the breaking point, and some might say beyond. But the landscape can shift if we drive toward a new set of values and behaviors. Investment cannot be the only tool, but it is one of the more ubiquitous representations of underlying value and values, and as such it embodies an opportunity to effect substantive change.

By directing resources away from social-value-subtracting firms, flexing shareholder power, and moving capital affirmatively toward positive enterprises, market-rate investment can play a great role in increasing equitability and sustainability on the global stage. And by channeling investment dollars into new, hybrid propositions that reimagine conventional risk and reward—and support community development, microfinance, and other social enterprises—we can drive a significant shift in equity and income to the world's poorest people.

To succeed, this blended value capital market will require a marked increase in the number and sophistication of a new generation of asset types, merchant bankers, and funds. These developments will need to be centered squarely upon facilitating participation by the legions of newly minted blended value investors.

By fully utilizing all financial resources, blended value investors and markets can create highly leveraged impact. It is a challenging proposition, to be sure—significant shifts from convention always are. But the more complete our early adoption, the better positioned we will be to accelerate broad-based change.

## References

Emerson, Jed. 2002. "Commentary: Horse Manure and Grantmaking." *Foundation News and Commentary*, May–June (www.foundationnews.org/CME/article.cfm?ID=1950).

Emerson, Jed, Timothy Freundlich, and Shari Berenbach. 2004. *The Investor's Toolkit: Generating Multiple Returns through a Unified Investment Strategy*. Draft available at www.ifc.org/ifcext/gbo.nsf/AttachmentsByTitle/Theinvestor'sToolkit/$FILE/The+Investor's+Toolkit.pdf.

Grameen Foundation USA. 2005. *Tapping Financial Markets for Microfinance*. Washington, D.C.

Khandker, Shahidur R., and Mark M. Pitt. 2002. "The Impact of Group-Based Credit on Poor Households: An Analysis of Panel Data from Bangladesh." Draft paper, World Bank, Washington.

Nelson Publications. 2003. *Nelson's Directory of Investment Managers*. Port Chester, N.Y.: Nelson Publications.

RISE (Research Initiative in Social Entrepreneurship). 2002. *RISE Capital Market Report: The Double Bottom Line Private Equity Landscape in 2002–2003*. New York: Columbia University Business School. Available at http://www.riseproject.org/uzrise_capmkt_rpt_03.pdf.

Social Investment Forum. 2003. *2003 Report on Socially Responsible Investing Trends in the United States*. Washington, D.C.

World Resources Institute and Merrill Lynch. 2005. *Energy Security and Climate Change: Investing in the Clean Car Revolution*. Washington, D.C.: World Resources Institute.

# 5

## *Should Government and Aid Agencies Subsidize Small Firms?*

Ross Levine

Should countries and international aid agencies subsidize small and medium-size enterprises (SMEs)? Subsidization can take many forms, including government guarantees, government-sponsored reductions in interest rates, and government-run directed-credit programs. Many argue that targeted assistance for SMEs is an effective strategy for spurring entrepreneurship, reducing poverty, lowering income inequality, and stimulating economic growth. Some skeptics, however, challenge this conclusion and argue that SMEs are at best a characteristic of successful countries, not a cause of that success.

The World Bank and other international financial institutions have clearly taken sides in this debate. For example, the World Bank Group approved more than $10 billion in SME support programs during the past five years. Furthermore, World Bank documents (World Bank 1994, 2002, 2004) suggest that this flow of support to SMEs is unlikely to abate. But is this a good strategy for fighting poverty? Could these funds reap greater development returns in other areas?

This chapter briefly reviews the arguments and empirical evidence for and against subsidizing SMEs. There are good conceptual arguments for all sides

Ross Levine is the Harrison S. Karvis University Professor in the Department of Economics at Brown University. His work focuses on the links between financial sector policies, the operation of financial systems, and economic growth. He has been a consultant for the World Bank, the International Monetary Fund, the Asian Development Bank, and the Inter-American Development Bank, among others.

of this debate and many points of convergence. Both SME advocates and skeptics agree that vibrant, private sector–oriented entrepreneurship is crucial for economic growth, poverty alleviation, and providing opportunities for people to fulfill their aspirations. Both agree that institutional failures stymie the emergence of new, innovative firms. Both agree that institutional failures promote and facilitate entrenchment, where privileged elites have unchallenged access to capital markets and business opportunities.

Yet they differ in terms of solutions. SME advocates believe direct subsidization programs for SMEs can help until there are improvements in the institutions. In contrast, SME skeptics emphasize that political failures are the source of institutional failures that strangle entrepreneurship and that these same political and institutional failures will undermine the effectiveness of government-run subsidization programs.

## The Pro-SME View

SME advocates make three core arguments. First, they argue that SMEs enhance competition and entrepreneurship and hence boost economy-wide efficiency and innovation. Intuitively, the entry of small firms—and the threat of new-firm entry—intensifies competition and productivity growth throughout the economy. Thus, direct government subsidization of SMEs will help countries exploit the social benefits of a more dynamic corporate sector.

Second, some SME supporters also argue that SMEs are more labor intensive than large firms. Expansion of the SME sector, therefore, will boost employment and hence reduce poverty. This suggests that subsidizing SMEs represents a tool for fighting poverty.

Third, SME proponents frequently claim that SMEs are more productive than large firms, but financial market and other institutional failures impede the formation and growth of SMEs. For example, some financial institutions funnel credit to well-established firms with whom they have long-standing relationships, rather than lending money to newer firms with better projects. This socially inefficient allocation of capital slows economic growth and discourages entrepreneurship. As another example, inefficient legal systems make it more costly and risky to use formal contracts to finance projects. This may lead financial systems to fund well-established, well-connected firms rather than relying on the formal contracting system to fund new firms with potentially high-return projects. Thus, poorly functioning legal systems encourage socially inefficient entrenchment: credit flows to the same firms based on historical and, in some cases, familial and political ties, rather than to those firms with the best projects.

From this perspective, direct government support to productive SMEs will improve the allocation of capital, boost economic growth, and give hope to aspiring entrepreneurs. Some critics retort that if the problem is poorly functioning financial and legal institutions, then the goal should be to fix these institutions; subsidizing SMEs is an ineffective and potentially counterproductive palliative. Pro-SME proponents, however, respond that it takes an exceptionally long time to build efficient institutions. Thus, from a practical perspective, governments can circumvent bad institutions and directly fund productivity-enhancing SMEs. Critically, this view assumes that government subsidization programs choose SMEs based on their expected social returns, not based on political connections or corruption.

## The Skeptical SME View

Skeptics challenge the efficacy of targeting assistance to SMEs. First, some analysts advertise the advantages of large firms relative to SMEs. In particular, large enterprises can exploit economies of scale and more easily undertake the large fixed costs associated with research and development. Thus, large firms are better than small firms at innovating and boosting productivity.

Second, skeptics challenge the assumption that SMEs are better for labor. Research finds that SMEs are neither more labor intensive nor better at job creation than large firms (Little, Mazumdar, and Page 1987). Indeed, some researchers find that large firms provide more stable, higher-quality jobs than small firms (Rosenzweig 1988). Furthermore, problems in financial, legal, and political systems may impede the ability of firms to grow to their most efficient size. Thus, a large number of SMEs may be a sign of a malfunctioning financial system, not a signal of vitality and innovative activity.

Third, some skeptics of the pro-SME view argue that policymakers should not focus on subsidizing SMEs but rather on improving the full range of institutions that affect the overall business environment. This involves removing barriers to the entry of new firms; lowering impediments to the exit of failing ones; reducing regulatory, tax, and other impediments to the efficient reallocation of labor; and enhancing the operation of legal and regulatory institutions that affect the financial system and business relations. Although these policies may boost SMEs, the goal is to make the business environment better for all firms, not to promote SMEs per se.

Fourth, critics of pro-SME policies argue that SME subsidization programs are likely to fail in exactly those economies where SMEs most need government subsidies to grow. The logic is as follows. Countries with poorly functioning political systems (closed, uncompetitive, autocratic political regimes) tend to also have poorly functioning legal and financial institutions. Poor legal and financial systems impede the flow of capital to SMEs and instead channel society's savings to established, politically connected firms. Thus, SMEs are most in need of government subsidies in countries with poor political systems. At the same time, however, poor political systems are unlikely to create subsidization programs that circumvent ineffective legal and financial systems and fund sound SMEs. This leads to the conclusion that where SMEs most need subsidies, SME subsidization is likely to operate ineffectively. At a broader level, in countries where small elites run the government, banks, and big industry, government-sponsored SME programs will have a low probability of funding the best firms from a social welfare perspective.

An example from history helps clarify this criticism of SME subsidization policies (Haber, Razo, and Maurer 2003). In the late nineteenth century, Porfirio Diaz solidified control of Mexico. To finance government expenditures with loans from banks, Diaz formed one huge bank, Banamex, and allowed the bankers to write the banking laws, which protected the banking system from competition. The board of directors of Banamex included the president of Congress, the under secretary of the Treasury, the senator for the Federal District, the president's chief of staff, and the brother of the secretary of the Treasury. Moreover, from 1886 to 1901, *all* the (nongovernmental) loans extended by Banamex went to the directors! In this type of political-financial system, government-run SME programs are unlikely to break the stranglehold on society's savings.

Fifth, skeptics question the validity of considering firm size as a determinant of economic success. For example, the natural resource endowments of a country may give it a comparative advantage in the production of goods that are made most economically by large firms (for example, steel). Another country may have natural and human resources that give it a technological advantage in producing products that are most efficiently made by small firms. Thus, the proportion of SMEs across countries may reflect differences in physical and human capital resources. From this perspective, pro-SME policies could actually distort firm size and potentially hurt economic efficiency.

## What the Evidence Suggests

Given the enormous amount of aid supporting SMEs around the world, there is surprisingly little evidence supporting this policy. Although Acs and Audretsch (1987) find that small firms have higher innovation rates in "high-technology," skill-intensive industries in the United States, Pagano and Schivardi (2001) show that a larger than average firm size is associated with faster innovation rates within Europe. In developing countries, technology transfers from abroad and imitation drive productivity improvement (Rosenberg 1976; Baumol 1994). Furthermore, research indicates that large exporting firms are typically the primary mechanism through which technologies are adapted from abroad to local circumstances. Thus, from a developing country perspective, the firm-level evidence does not favor SME subsidization as a mechanism for boosting innovation and productivity growth. (This literature review borrows liberally, without further attribution, from my paper with Thorsten Beck and Asli Demirgüç-Kunt [Beck, Demirgüç-Kunt, and Levine 2005], which contains additional references.)

Similarly, although early work by Birch (1979) argued that small firms are particularly important for job creation, subsequent research has refuted this conclusion. As noted above, microeconomic evidence does not robustly conclude that SMEs boost employment or provide better jobs. Although pro-SME advocates claim that SMEs stimulate competition, innovation, and productivity growth to a greater degree than large firms, the evidence is at best inconclusive.

Instead, an emerging body of research finds that firm size responds to the functioning of national financial and legal systems. For instance, Beck, Demirgüç-Kunt, and Maksimovic (2003) demonstrate that financial development eases financial constraints on successful firms and allows them to grow. Kumar, Rajan, and Zingales (2001) show that countries with better legal systems—legal systems that more efficiently enforce private contracts—tend to have larger firms. Because financial and legal institutions affect SMEs, large firms, and the distribution of firms in the economy, these findings indicate that policymakers should not view SMEs as engines, where pouring in more subsidies fosters growth and alleviates poverty. Instead, this work sheds the policy reform spotlight on regulatory and legal reforms that improve the functioning of financial and legal systems.

Finally, Beck, Demirgüç-Kunt, and Levine (2005) provide cross-country evidence on whether SMEs boost economic growth, alleviate poverty, and reduce income inequality. They find a strong, positive association between the size of the SME sector and the rate of economic growth. But they do not find that SMEs cause growth. Furthermore, the comparisons do not indicate that SMEs exert a particularly beneficial impact on poverty or income distribution. Although a prosperous SME sector is a characteristic of flourishing economies, the evidence does not support the pro-SME prescription of directly subsidizing SME development to accelerate growth and reduce poverty. Moreover, even if these studies had found that SMEs cause growth, this would not necessarily support subsidization of SMEs. These studies examine the connection between the SME sector and economic outcomes, not the connection between government subsidies of SMEs and economic outcomes. Because there are serious doubts about whether government-sponsored support programs for SMEs will reach the best firms, this creates further doubts about the efficacy of subsidizing SMEs.

In sum, the econometric evidence does not validate a policy of subsidizing SMEs. Thus, funds currently being devoted to subsidizing SMEs might have a bigger impact on economic development if used elsewhere.

## The Importance of the Political System

In this last section, I briefly discuss the links between the political system, policies toward the financial systems, the operation of banks, and why this is relevant for the SME debate. The goal of this section is to take a step back from SMEs per se and emphasize the broader context in which policymakers need to contemplate reforms that will allow the private sector to operate more efficiently and reduce poverty.

Joseph Schumpeter (1912)—considered by many to be the father of development economics—argues that the banker acts in the name of society when authorizing the entrepreneur to innovate. His point is that the financial system mobilizes savings and decides who gets to use these savings. This is a crucial decision. If the financial system identifies and finances entrepreneurs with sound projects, this fosters innovation and economic prosperity. If the financial system funnels credit to friends and cronies, then this discourages entrepreneurship and thwarts economic development. Thus, the financial system is crucial because it distributes society's savings.

Because the financial system influences who is able to start or expand a business and who does not, financial sector policies attract the attention of the economically and politically powerful. For example, in the early decades of the United States, the Federalists granted banking licenses to Federalists, not to Republicans. The government used public policies to funnel society's savings to political constituents. When the Republicans gained control of the federal and state governments, they quickly granted banking licenses to their supporters. The emergence of new banks increased competition and allowed a broader set of entrepreneurs to compete for scarce capital. It was only through political competition that the United States enjoyed competition within the financial system. Thus, greater political competition facilitated a more efficient allocation of resources and hence faster economic growth.

The idea that the political system influences financial sector policies is supported by cross-country evidence presented in a new book I have written with James Barth and Gerard Caprio (Barth, Caprio, and Levine 2006). Open, competitive, democratic political systems tend to choose financial sector policies that encourage the entry of new banks, foster greater competition among financial institutions, and grant less of a role to government-owned banks. In contrast, countries with more autocratic, less open, and uncompetitive political systems choose financial sector policies that protect existing banks and reduce competition in capital markets.

This is not surprising. Sound financial sector policies funnel capital to projects with the highest expected returns, which may subvert the interests of powerful segments of society. Consequently, these powerful interests frequently use their political influence to enact rules and regulations that thwart competition and help maintain the status quo.

Because the political system influences financial sector policies, which in turn influence how banks and other segments of the financial system allocate capital, this line of argument stresses that understanding the role of SMEs in an economy cannot be usefully disentangled from that country's political institutions. Competitive, open political systems are likely to produce regulations and legal systems that foster competition in the financial system that lead to an efficient allocation of capital. In this context, there is little need for direct subsidization of SMEs. More closed, autocratic political systems are likely to select regulations and legal systems that impede competition in the financial sector and that funnel credit toward politically attractive ends. In this context, there are serious questions about whether government-sponsored and -managed subsidization programs will circumvent political pressures and direct credit toward promising SMEs.

## References

Acs, Zoltan J., and David B. Audretsch. 1987. "Innovation, Market Structure, and Firm Size." *Review of Economics and Statistics* 69: 567–74.

Barth, James, Gerard Caprio, and Ross Levine. 2006. *Rethinking Bank Regulation: Till Angels Govern*. Cambridge University Press.

Baumol, William J. 1994. *Entrepreneurship, Management, and the Structure of Payoffs*. MIT Press.

Beck, Thorsten, Asli Demirgüç-Kunt, and Ross Levine. 2005. "SMEs, Growth, and Poverty." *Journal of Economic Growth* 10: 199–229.

Beck, Thorsten, Asli Demirgüç-Kunt, and Vojislav Maksimovic. 2003. "Financial and Legal Institutions and Firm Size." Washington, D.C.: World Bank. Mimeo.

Birch, David L. 1979. *The Job Generation Process: Final Report to Economic Development Administration*. Cambridge, Mass.: MIT Program on Neighborhood and Regional Change.

Haber, Stephen, Armando Razo, and Noel Maurer. 2003. *The Politics of Property Rights: Political Instability, Credible Commitments, and Economic Growth in Mexico*. Cambridge University Press.

Kumar, Krishna B., Raghuram, G. Rajan, and Luigi Zingales. 2001. "What Determines Firm Size?" Working Paper 496. Chicago: Center for Research in Security Prices, University of Chicago.

Little, Ian M. D., Dipak Mazumdar, and John M. Page Jr. 1987. *Small Manufacturing Enterprises: A Comparative Analysis of India and Other Economies*. Oxford University Press.

Pagano, Patrizio, and Fabiano Schivardi. 2001. "Firm Size Distribution and Growth." Working Paper 394. Rome: Banca d'Italia.

Rosenberg, Nathan. 1976. *Perspectives on Technology*. Cambridge University Press.

Rosenzweig, Mark R. 1988. "Labor Markets in Low-Income Countries." In *Handbook of Development Economics*, vol. 1, edited by Hollis B. Chenery and T. N. Srinivasan. Amsterdam: North-Holland.

Schumpeter, Joseph A. 1912. *The Theory of Economic Development*. Translated by R. Opie. Reprint, Harvard University Press, 1934.

World Bank. 1994. *Can Intervention Work? The Role of Government in SME Success*. Washington, D.C.

———. 2002. *Review of Small Business Activities*. Washington, D.C.

———. 2004. *Review of Small Business Activities*. Washington, D.C.

# 6

## *Venture Capital for Development*

ALAN J. PATRICOF AND JULIE E. SUNDERLAND

THE DEVELOPING WORLD, and Africa in particular, faces a dearth of risk capital that has constrained and will continue to constrain growth. Donors need to face the reality that the young companies that can really move the needle on innovation, inspiration, and employment need high-risk, reasonably sized equity investments to grow, not the limited doles of short-term, high-interest debt currently provided.

In the developed world, the young growth companies critical to innovative capacity and employment generation are financed with long-term, permanent equity capital. When a company is growing rapidly, it cannot generate sufficient cash through its current operations to support the investment

Alan J. Patricof is the cofounder of Apax Partners, Inc., one of the world's leading private equity firms, with operations in eight countries and more than $12 billion under management. He is also a member of the UNDP Commission on the Private Sector and Development and the Council on Foreign Relations, where he is a member of the Committee on Corporate Affairs.

Julie E. Sunderland is a consultant on private sector development, especially small business development and financing, to development finance institutions, governments, and fund managers. She is currently working with the African Development Foundation to expand its SME investment activities in Africa and the IFC's Global Business School Network to improve business education and training in Africa. She has published a number of articles on private equity in emerging markets and SME support programs.

Both authors have worked closely with leading small and medium-size enterprise funds, including evaluating the underlying portfolios of the funds and the key factors affecting returns. The authors wish to acknowledge the support of these fund managers in contributing to the development of the ideas in this chapter.

required to generate future growth, nor can it afford to pay current interest or amortize the principal associated with loans. Angel investors and venture capitalists provide the equity capital that enables young businesses to take risks, build plants, develop technology, and implement their long-term strategies to compete on a global basis.

Yet companies in the poorest countries of the world have almost no access to this type of capital. Entrepreneurs struggle to build businesses with meager personal assets that rarely allow them to achieve the scale of operations required to be competitive. When entrepreneurs can get a loan—the only form of financing available in the market—the requirement to service the capital on a current basis puts undue pressure on their balance sheet, their ability to reinvest in the growth of their business, and their willingness to take risks.

This past year has seen a renewed call to action to address persistent poverty in the developing world, especially in Africa. The key message from most of the discussions has been a call for an increase in development aid. But just spending more money is not going to build the long-term functional economies that will create the employment and wealth to get poor African nations and other poor countries out of their poverty trap. We need to get money into the hands of entrepreneurs who can build the businesses to enhance Africa's global competitive advantage and produce goods and services affordable to the world's poor people.

We propose a specific program, an equity investment initiative funded by donors, which can have a real impact on business formation in the developing world. In partnership with local governments and investors, the program would provide equity capital and technical assistance to the subset of young small and medium-size enterprises (SMEs) in developing countries that are truly growth oriented and that the capital markets are not adequately supporting. These suggestions are offered as a beginning, not an end; any initiative must strive to create viable private capital markets over time that can provide appropriate commercial instruments with reasonable financial rewards.

## Growth Matters More Than Size

The current landscape of companies in Africa and in poor countries and their requirements for capital and assistance are most often described in terms of the size of companies. The "microenterprise" sector is typically defined as companies with fewer than ten employees and generally includes small-scale traders, artisanal producers, and farmers. Increasingly, these types of enterprises have been provided with capital and technical assistance by the burgeoning and successful microfinance industry. The "large" enterprise sector is typically defined as anything with more than 100 employees and therefore includes multinationals and almost all established local companies such as privatized infrastructure providers and financial institutions. In most cases, local and international capital markets provide these types of companies with the necessary capital. The in-between SME sector, however, remains both the life-blood of the economy and the most challenging for policymakers to understand and financiers—whether commercial or donor—to serve. (Size definitions vary by country and organization; SMEs are typically defined as companies with fewer than 100, 250, or 500 employees. As noted above, microenterprises are typically defined as those with fewer than ten employees.).

This one-size-fits-all categorization of companies with between ten and 100 or more employees as SMEs hides variations in characteristics that are critical to their capital and assistance needs and their potential development impact. Most of the companies in the SME-size category in developing countries are similar to microenterprises in that they provide basic employment and income generation for a family or farming cooperative group. Because these types of "necessity entrepreneurs"—traders, niche domestic service providers, and agricultural producer groups—are oriented toward generating immediate income, they are unlikely to have or to be able to reinvest capital in their businesses and take risks to grow significantly. As a result, these types of enterprises are unlikely to reach an economic scale to become globally competitive. However, they can also usually generate enough cash flow to service some form of debt. Many access working capital or trade finance through informal networks, and a number of specialized providers of debt financing for this type of company have recently emerged.

A smaller segment of companies in this SME category, including high potential start-ups, have the capacity to grow and become modern, globally competitive enterprises. These types of companies are run by "opportunity entrepreneurs" committed to innovating, adding value to exports, applying technology, achieving scale in production, and reinvesting profit in their businesses. And like their U.S. counterparts, they can have a *multiplier effect* on employment and overall economic growth. If these companies are successful in growing and reinvesting capital in their businesses, they can continue to expand direct employment, increase indirect income generation through sourcing local inputs, and pay taxes. (A 1996 study of California, for example, showed that 3 to 4 percent of total firms termed "Gazelles" had a growth in sales of 20 percent from a base revenue of $100,000 and generated a *majority* of new jobs; see Koehler and Moller 1998.) Perhaps as important, successful companies and entrepreneurs can have a powerful demonstration impact:

seeding and stabilizing clusters of related firms, inspiring other entrepreneurs to grow their businesses, and serving as role models for youth. Unlike their "necessity entrepreneur" sisters and brethren, the impact of the capital invested in growth-oriented SMEs run by "opportunity entrepreneurs" can continue to have a compounding development impact.

But unlike in the United States and other developed economies, in most developing countries these segments of growth-oriented SMEs are virtually absent. (The Global Entrepreneurship Monitor, www.gemconsortium.org, every year undertakes a survey of entrepreneurship in thirty-nine countries and actively uses the concept of "necessity" and "opportunity" entrepreneurs in its surveys to distinguish between voluntary pursuit of an attractive business opportunity and those acting out of necessity. It notes that opportunity entrepreneurs dominate in developed countries while necessity entrepreneurs are up to half of those involved in developing countries.) In high-income countries, the SME sector has been estimated to contribute more than 50 percent to gross domestic product (GDP), not to mention being the engine of new job creation and a source of as much as half the innovation in these economies. In low-income countries, however, the contribution of the SME sector to GDP has been estimated at 16 percent, and in most African countries the SME sector has been estimated at less than 10 percent (Meghana, Demirgüç-Kunt, and Beck 2003). This absent segment of companies that are undergoing the risky but creative process of growing from small to medium size to large could explain much of the weakness in the overall economic growth of developing countries.

There are three basic explanations for the underdevelopment of the SME sector in developing countries: a weak business environment, a lack of managerial or technical capacity, and a lack of access to capital. We will not attempt to explain all three factors but will focus on the access to capital for growth-oriented SMEs (for a full discussion of all three factors, see Patricof and Sunderland 2005). It should be noted, however, that without progress by local governments in creating an investment climate and business environment that are supportive of entrepreneurship and growth-oriented businesses, any policies related to increasing access to capital for SMEs will have limited impact.

## Risk-Reward Imbalances

In developed country environments, young companies are financed by various types of risk capital providers through a number of rounds of investment: friends and family supplying very early capital, angel investors such as retired businessmen providing start-up capital, and formal venture capitalists providing early-stage and growth capital. Each of these types of investors has specialized skills and information to evaluate the risks and rewards of the business plan at each stage of investment and to help the entrepreneur build the business. By the time a successful young company has graduated out of this risk capital market, it should have the cash flow or track record to access more formal capital markets such as banks and public markets. These public markets and mergers and acquisitions activity provide the critical high potential exit for the early risk capital providers.

Almost all developing countries lack this early risk capital market. This does not reflect neglect from development experts at the development finance institutions (DFIs). Surveys of the SME sector in developing countries have consistently identified a lack of access to capital as a key constraint on growth. (There are numerous region- and country-specific surveys of the dynamics of the SME sector and constraints on growth; for a recent general evaluation of the SME sector in fifty-four countries, see Beck, Demirgüç-Kunt, and Maksimovic 2005.) In response, during the past two decades, a range of schemes—from direct investments in the SME sector to venture capital programs and SME loan guarantee programs—have been attempted.

Most of these DFI-funded programs, however, have had limited success. Loan programs have often suffered from a lack of utilization by the SME sector, high default rates, and currency devaluations. Equity investments in SMEs through the nascent private equity and venture capital industry have generated mostly poor returns and many business failures. As evidenced in recently gathered data on the emerging market private equity industry, private equity funds in emerging markets (including a mix of both venture capital and larger private equity transactions) have globally only returned capital to investors, delivering a –0.3 percent internal rate of return over a five- to ten-year horizon. Venture capital investments have been shown to be even more difficult to manage. Data from the European Bank for Reconstruction and Development's (EBRD's) analysis of its funds in Eastern Europe show that investments of less than $2.5 million did not even return capital, while investments greater than $10 million delivered returns significantly above the emerging market private equity benchmark.[1]

1. Statistical performance data from Cambridge Associates Emerging Market Venture Capital and Private Equity Index have only recently been made publicly available; see *Emerging Market Private Equity Newsletter* 1, no. 2, June 2005, for a summary of the data. The EBRD analysis of the performance of its investment funds between 1992 and 2002 was presented in detail at the IFC Global Annual Private Equity Conference in May 2004; general performance data for the EBRD-sponsored funds are available at www.ebrd.com/country/sector/fi/index.htm.

For investments of less than $250,000, the challenges to delivering net returns to investors become even greater. Analyzing the portfolios of leading global SME funds shows that, without even taking into account transaction costs, the gross realizations and valuations on these investments barely return capital to the funds, compared with healthier multiples on larger investments. When even small transaction costs are incorporated into the returns' calculations, the base capital on the small investments is quickly eroded.

The result of these historical returns is that commercial investors in developing countries necessarily migrate toward larger deals. Even the leading global SME funds, reacting to pressure from their primarily DFI investor base to demonstrate commercial returns, have increasingly abandoned smaller SME equity investments and migrated toward minimum-size investments from $500,000 to $1 million, and most frequently to $2 million, with a large component of their investments structured as interest-bearing securities.

With the renewed focus on private sector development and the importance placed on the SME sector, however, the development finance industry is desperately seeking a scalable solution for delivering capital to the SME sector. As evidenced in the returns data, the difficulty with such a model is that, in most cases, the challenges of building growth-oriented companies in these markets mean that equity investments cannot deliver returns that justify the risks on a commercial basis. There are a number of reasons for this.

*Early stage of investment.* In many of the most promising developing countries, a stabilized economy and adequately functioning business environments have only been a condition of the past decade. Unless a product of privatization, companies with a high growth potential will often be start-ups or early-stage companies with unproven products and marketing strategies and limited track records. Investing in start-ups is notoriously difficult and risky—even commercial venture capitalists in the sophisticated U.S. market like to have some proof of a business plan and as a result leave the earliest stages of investment to angel investors.

*Weak managerial capacity.* Many developing countries have extraordinary raw entrepreneurial talent—as evidenced in the traders who effectively move large flows of goods across borders. But building and managing a modern enterprise that can add value and compete in international markets require significantly different business language, contacts, and technical skills to which few of these raw entrepreneurs have access. For example, the stringent needs for quality control and timely delivery on contracts can be challenging for a businessperson accustomed to the chaotic African trading environment.

*Business environment risks.* In addition to the usual risks of starting and growing a company, these entrepreneurs must battle the hurdles created by government regulation, infrastructure weaknesses, and even cultural impediments. Studies have shown that weaknesses in the business environment disproportionately affect smaller businesses (see Beck, Demirgüç-Kunt, and Maksimovic 2005; for a discussion of the relationship between firm growth, failure rates, and macroeconomic conditions, see Mead and Liedholm 1998). What these studies do not adequately convey is the day-to-day drain on resources and morale of dealing with issues such as official corruption, power outages, lack of communication, and poor roads that destroy vehicles and increase delivery times.

*Few exit opportunities.* Though local capital markets have been established in many developing countries, they have thus far been open primarily to large and established companies. The mergers and acquisitions market in most of these markets also remains nascent. Therefore, with limited possibility for exits from equity investments, investors have focused on debt instruments that are appropriate only for companies that generate cash flow.

*High transaction costs and limited deal flow.* For the investors themselves, investing in the SME sector presents difficult challenges. Investing in a small company takes many if not more resources than a larger transaction. Furthermore, the scale of most of these markets means that there just is not, at this point in time, the potential to create that many high-growth-oriented companies in any given country. As a result, the overhead costs involved in setting up an investment operation can be extremely high on a per deal basis.

*Currency risk.* For international investors, currency volatility can further erode returns. Many investments generating a positive return produce negative or minimal returns when converted to U.S. dollars.

These factors make SME investing in growth-oriented companies in developing countries difficult, if not impossible, to justify in commercial terms. The companies themselves are most often at an early stage under any definition, with unproven and inexperienced entrepreneurs. The markets in which they operate exacerbate the companies' risks. Even if the companies are successful, the rewards are difficult to achieve. The investor will have trouble getting liquidity from the investment, and the transaction and overhead costs associated with investment management activity further erode the returns.

Without some form of balancing incentive, therefore, commercial investors who expect returns to justify their risks are not likely to invest in the SME sector in these countries in the near future. At the same time, to meet the financial objectives established by their shareholders, most of the

DFI investors continue to demand commercial-level returns from SME investing. Because their incentive structure often rewards large top-line disbursements of capital, the DFI investors also rarely get excited by the volume of capital appropriate to the SME segment.

This does not mean that DFI investors should abandon the sector. Rather, it is time for the DFI investors to be realistic about what effective investing in this sector really takes and to adjust their thinking and benchmarks accordingly. We strongly believe that if the DFI community wants to build young, growth-oriented SMEs in these markets, they will need to accept the risk-reward imbalance and begin to promote models for SME investing that take into account the high risks, high transaction costs, low volume, and below-market rates of return endemic to the sector.

## A Balancing Act

This type of reorientation in approach sounds simple in concept but is difficult to execute in practice because it requires a careful balancing act between creating market-driven incentives that enforce commercial discipline at the investment and company level and achieving the development objective of building businesses. Distorting capital markets with too much cheap capital or creating uncompetitive companies is always a danger when providing below-market funding to the private sector. Therefore, over time, any initiative must strive to create viable private capital markets that can provide appropriate commercial instruments with reasonable financial rewards.

We propose, therefore, a program to create a pool of capital to invest equity or equity-like instruments in growth-oriented SMEs. The funds would, as much as possible in a given market, seek to leverage and build the nascent commercial risk capital market. This program would include:

*Capitalization.* Capital for the funds would be sourced from DFI investors, from local governments, and, crucially, with some participation, however modest, from private local sources. The donor investors and governments should be willing to accept very modest rates of return and directly support operating and transaction costs, allowing local private investors to manage the investments and take a disproportionate amount of the returns.

*Investment activities.* Capital from these funds should be available in amounts ranging from $100,000 to $2 million to invest in SMEs with the demonstrated ability to absorb capital and a growth strategy that can have a multiplier effect on employment. Investments should be in the form of quasi equity with no forced amortization or current servicing required. Investors will receive returns from appreciation in the value of equity ownership where possible but more often in the form of payments linked to participation in increased revenues and free cash flow as generated.

*Technical assistance.* Capital alone will not be enough to develop growth-oriented SMEs in these markets. These companies need management training, advice from experienced businesspeople, technical knowledge of equipment and processes, market information, and insights to build their businesses. A parallel component of the funds will be dedicated to funding for technical and managerial assistance to the portfolio companies through existing assistance programs. The technical and managerial assistance component of the program should be fully integrated into the investment activities. This type of assistance will be provided on a full grant basis so as not to have a material impact on the overall investment return.

*Commitment of the companies.* The companies themselves will also need to be active participants in the program; in exchange for capital and technical assistance, they would commit to produce audited statements, pay taxes, and abide by the rules of corporate governance.

*Linking with the diaspora.* The flow of entrepreneurs from the Indian and Chinese diasporas has had a significant impact on the quality of the young companies in those economies. The African diaspora has also begun to generate both the capital and the entrepreneurs that could significantly boost the SME sector's potential. The program should provide incentives for investment by the diaspora communities, encourage diaspora entrepreneurs to develop new companies in their home countries, and involve senior businesspeople from the diaspora in the program.

*Investment skills.* If local investors have appropriate skills and knowledge, they are much more likely to understand the risks and rewards of the SME sector and will be better placed to manage them on a day-to-day basis. Pairing local investors with skilled international fund managers could transfer the necessary knowledge and skills. Involving experienced venture capitalists in the overall management of the program should also allow for transfer of knowledge and skills.

*Linkages to pure commercial markets.* In addition to being managed by local private investors, the funds should work closely with other local financial institutions to graduate their companies for later-stage financing from purely commercial sources. This could be achieved through prefinancing of companies referred by the banking sector, working closely with banks to get loan financing for existing portfolio companies, and co-investing at later stages of financing with commercial venture capital funds.

The program will need to be adapted to the on-the-ground characteristics of the SME sector, the human resources, and the financial markets in a given country or region. Equity capital is not a one-size-fits-all solution for the SME sector. In fact, in smaller or less-developed countries, it may only be appropriate for a few companies. Regional funds therefore may be appropriate for regions with fragmented local markets and a limited deal flow. The risks associated with the investments will also vary by the characteristics of the macroeconomy and the financial markets. Smaller investments with higher leverage rates may be needed in underdeveloped markets, whereas larger investments with lower leverage rates may be acceptable in more developed markets.

Nonetheless, the proposal aims to specifically address the returns challenge in the commercial SME investing market by significantly leveraging returns to local private investors to offset the substantial risks outlined in the previous section: early stage of investment, business environment, managerial deficiency, and currency risks. Until capital markets are stronger, exiting investments will always be a challenge; however, with adequate leverage and use of some of the quasi-equity instruments described above, investors should be able to generate cash flow from investments without destroying the growth potential of their investments. Finally, the integration of technical assistance on a grant basis, the commitment from target companies to enhance transparency and governance, and the diaspora links will strengthen the potential for success of the underlying SME investments as small business owners learn and adopt the management practices of the modern, global enterprises.

In the long term, this proposal's greatest success will be in developing a fully commercial local venture capital industry in which leverage from DFIs and government is no longer necessary. By proactively transferring investment knowledge, by demanding participation from local investors, and by encouraging linkages to the existing commercial sector, the proposal will support local investors in learning how to assess and manage the risks of SME investing and in beginning to behave like true venture capital investors.

## Conclusion

In all the discussion of aid and poverty, we sometimes lose sight of the fact that enabling poor people to not be poor requires employment and preferably employment sustained by productive economic activity rather than capricious donor funding. Foreign direct investment can provide some of this employment, and microenterprise activity can support basic income generation. But a vibrant, indigenous private sector presents the best prospect for enduring progress in creating the employment and wealth that will pull Africa and other poor countries out of poverty. A "private sector," however, does not spontaneously emerge from the pages of commission and consultant reports. Rather, young businesses must grow to become the larger, established institutions that can really move the needle on employment.

Apple Computer, Microsoft, and FedEx did not start out with loans. If their founders had been required to finance their early growth with the short-term, collateralized, high-interest loans currently available in developing countries, the businesses would not even have gotten off the ground. Instead, friends and family, angel investors, venture capitalists, and even the U.S. government's Small Business Administration provided risk capital to build these successful U.S. companies.

In developing countries, we must similarly find a way to get equity capital into the hands of entrepreneurs who have the capacity to build young businesses. We believe our program provides a good place to start.

## References

Beck, T., A. Demirgüç-Kunt, and V. Maksimovic. 2005. "Financial and Legal Constraints to Growth: Does Size Matter?" *Journal of Finance* 60, no. 1: 137–70.

Koehler, Gus, and Rosa Maria Moller. 1998. *Business Capital Needs in California*. Sacramento: California Research Bureau.

Mead, Donald C., and Carl Liedholm. 1998. "The Dynamics of Micro and Small Enterprises in Developing Countries." *World Development* 26, no. 1: 61–74.

Meghana, Ayyagari, Asli Demirgüç-Kunt, and Thorsten Beck. 2003. "Small and Medium Enterprises across the Globe: A New Database." World Bank Policy Research Working Paper 3127. Washington, D.C.: World Bank.

Patricof, A., and J. Sunderland. 2005. "Big Ideas: Small Is Still Beautiful." *Milken Institute Review* (June): 90–94.

# 7

# *Innovative Financing Options and the Fight against Global Poverty: What's New and What Next?*

DAVID DE FERRANTI

CAN INNOVATIVE APPROACHES to mobilizing and utilizing financial resources make a difference in the fight against global poverty? Potentially yes, this chapter argues—but with a caveat. To get from "potentially" to "certainly" will require much more practical experience with, and careful assessment of, the best of the emerging proposals, few of which have been adequately tested in action thus far.

Further, many proposals, including some that are presently much touted, may not survive this implementation test. Only a few may, in the end, merit full scaling up. Also, though a few may make noticeable contributions, none is likely to totally revolutionize the long, hard work of development; there is no silver bullet in the offing. New approaches can be useful additions to the current array of instruments and activities for helping developing countries, but will not be so broadly applicable and effective that the present mainstays will be replaced or needed less.

And finally, the innovations that have the biggest payoffs will draw especially on private sector channels, either exclusively or, more likely, in partnership with public sector and multilateral channels. The background for this issue is discussed first below, then an overview of the options is provided,

David de Ferranti is a senior fellow at the Brookings Institution. He worked at the World Bank for two decades, most recently as head of the Latin America and the Caribbean group. Previously, he conducted and directed policy research on U.S. domestic programs at the RAND Corporation.

various ways of thinking about them are outlined, and, finally, three specific options are examined.

## Why This Issue and Why Now

Interest in finding new and better ways to facilitate development—and proposals for how to do so—is not new. Nor are the main reasons for constantly seeking improved solutions. Basically, anything that can result in more progress and leverage the limited available resources more effectively is beneficial both for the countries concerned and for the international community of institutions seeking to help them.

Lately, discussion of this subject, and of particular options that appear especially promising, has become much more prominent. There are several reasons for this, and they are important here because they go to the heart of questions that are fundamental for any investigation of possible new approaches to anything. Those questions are: What are the overall objectives being sought? What would the new options be aimed at achieving? Why are the existing options not sufficient? And what would a change from old to new options be expected to produce in benefits (after also taking into account the costs of the change)?

One reason for the heightened search now for new options is that the current situation is widely felt to be inadequate. The prevailing levels of financial flows for development, domestically within developing countries and externally from donors and other partners, and the current mechanisms and practices for mobilizing and utilizing those flows are seen to be insufficient to meet the needs of developing countries to reduce poverty and achieve higher levels of development at the pace that they and the international community would like. Business as usual—it has often been said, whether at Monterrey, Group of Eight (G-8) meetings, or countless other "summits"—will not be enough to tackle critical problems fast enough.

There is some truth to these concerns. Calculations of aid flows in relation to the spending levels required to attain substantial progress invariably show large shortfalls. Among the many areas that feel the pinch, key health threats such as HIV/AIDS and malaria are outrunning efforts to contain them.

A closely related further consideration is that "official development assistance"—the public sector part of total flows—is not only too limited to meet the need but has also recently been cause for some concern because these flows may drift downward rather than move upward in the years ahead. Exceptions like Sweden, which has just transitioned to a commitment to increase its aid substantially so as to reach 1 percent of its gross domestic product, are more positive. However, close watchers of U.S., European, and other flows from countries belonging to the Organization for Economic Cooperation and Development, and the intricate politics behind them, including the shifting views of voters, are less optimistic. Some note that recent proposals such as France's ideas on global taxation of air travel and Gordon Brown's International Finance Facility may have emerged at least in part from concern that conventional aid flows would come under downward pressure as voters and their representatives rethought their priorities. U.S. flows, though up notably under the current administration, seem always to be at risk of falling.

An additional consideration is related to the private sector's part of total flows. Private flows, which are primarily for investment and other commercial purposes though with a smaller but influential addition of philanthropic funds as well, greatly dwarf public aid, as is often noted. Private flows help promote development in multiple ways, principally through the impact that investment has on economic activity, employment, incomes, and opportunities for entrepreneurs. Yet their impact is also limited by the fact that the bulk of them go to just the most attractive countries and sectors. They typically have not done much for crucial areas for development that do not provide attractive financial returns, such as education and health.

The obvious question that many have thus asked, especially recently and in light of the growing awareness that public flows are likely to remain highly constrained for the foreseeable future, is whether private flows can somehow evolve in directions that can be of more help to development. This might be either through simply expanding current flows or through enticing providers of funds to reach places and activities that have benefited little in the past. These thoughts have led, in turn, to sharpened curiosity about what sorts of tools might do just that and thus whether innovative financing instruments might be needed and might actually help.

Adding to all these factors has been another issue: the growing dissatisfaction with the lack of more and better results from efforts to support development. Participants around the world in the aid and development business—from citizens to the many organizations involved—are concerned about "development effectiveness." The unfortunate confluence of new generations of players coming to the scene and larger geopolitical sea changes, together with excessive promises for how much could be accomplished by when and too few successes and too many conspicuous and spectacular failures, has soured many on everything connected with things as they are. Hopes for better progress—and strong passion behind it—have inevitably reinforced interest in seeking new ways of doing things, including in how the funding for development is done.

Moreover, the changing landscape of the global and local challenges that need attention and the participants' appreciation and priorities among them have also fueled the search for innovative financing. Global public goods (such as the discovery of new vaccines for major diseases) and public "bads" (the unfolding of the HIV/AIDS pandemic) require different kinds of responses from the older, more traditional struggles to build schools or improve water systems.

Inevitably, given the diversity of these and yet further factors, the question of what the objective is in considering possible new approaches has no simple answer, as the next section further illustrates. Clearly, though, the guiding principle for deciding which options deserve the most attention is which would produce the most net benefits after taking into account the associated costs, including any transition costs. This, however, is no easy task, as will be apparent below.

## What Are the Options? A Brief Introductory Tour

The options for new approaches that come up most often for discussion are currently both numerous (one can readily list at least twenty-five) and diverse (ranging from purely public sector to purely private sector initiatives, with a raft of mixed schemes in between). Box 7-1 lists several of them.

Among the purely public sector options, one category encompasses new forms of taxation, the most prominent example being the French proposal, mentioned above, for taxing air travel (or more precisely, the fuel for air travel) in some internationally fair way. Another category, of which Gordon Brown's International Finance Facility (IFF) is the best known, involves borrowing against future aid flows so that resources that can do the most good today rather than tomorrow can in fact be used today. Using securitization and the bond markets, the IFF concept would be most helpful for activities—such as controlling a serious disease—where more action in the near term is vital rather than spreading out a program evenly over all years indefinitely.

A third category concentrates solely on certain health issues, and unlike the previous two, which are entirely public sector actions, links public and private actions together. This category could in principle be readily extended to other areas, even outside the health sector (for instance, to environmental protection), but has not been thus far, mostly because the donors and other

BOX 7-1

**A Plethora of Ideas and Proposals**

- Global taxes (for example, for air tickets)
- International finance facility (IFF)
- Advance purchase commitments
- Targeted exclusions from patent rights
- Tax relief for donating key medicines
- Market interventions for key medicines
- Debt buydowns (for example, as in the polio campaign)
- Results-based sequences of loans/grants
- Local currency lending
- Guarantees from bilaterals or IFIs
- Infrastructure guarantee facility
- Risk insurance for natural disasters
- Other risk insurance (for example, crop prices)
- Debt relief (HIPCs, G-8 2005, and beyond)
- Global development bonds
- Long-term sustainable investing (generation)
- Private equity investing with enhancements
- Angel/patient equity investing (SMEs or GBOs)
- Tripartite venture capital firms (Rotberg)
- Microfinance (and tiers of support to it)
- Microenterprise development
- Blended value investing (for example, Domini)
- Social investment partnerships (from GEXSI)
- Enhanced management of voluntary giving
- Electronic-billing-based fundraising
- Remittances (and derivatives from them)
- "Use your balance sheet more" (for IFIs)
- "Use your endowment more" (for philanthropy)

Note: SMEs = small and medium-size enterprises; GBOs = grassroots business organizations; IFIs = international financial institutions; HIPCs = highly indebted poor countries; G-8 = Group of Eight.

partners backing the proposals have a strong focus on their own strategic priorities in health and, within health, on the major diseases with high morbidity and mortality implications that are the target of the current proposals.

Among the specific ideas on health options is a reduced version of the IFF aimed at encouraging investment in vaccine development and immunization. This "IFFIm" is slated to be in full flight soon. Another idea is the Advance Purchase Commitment, which would be aimed at strengthening incentives for private sector–led research and development to generate effective vaccines against malaria and possibly other diseases as well. Still another, referred to here as Targeted Exclusions from Patent Rights, would seek to enable developing countries to get more affordable access to selected medicines without hurting the producers (because those countries would not purchase them otherwise, given their high cost under patent). And another, Tax Relief for Donating Key Medicines, would focus on possible changes in U.S. tax rules that would make it more attractive to U.S. producers to donate more to developing countries (there apparently are ways of doing this that would not cost the United States much in terms of lost revenue). Finally, Market Interventions for Key Medicines would team up the funds of interested parties and the power of the marketplace to ensure sufficient demand for especially important medicines to elicit and sustain adequate supply.

A fourth category, which could be either a totally public sector play or a combined public and private undertaking, builds upon two ideas, one from polio eradication efforts and the other from the growing chorus of voices insisting on getting results from aid—that is, performance-based support. In the polio case, the idea of "debt buydowns" linked loans by the World Bank with up-front commitments by donors to pay off the loans, thus enabling the recipient country to have the funds it needed, from the start, to tackle polio but without a long-term buildup in its debt burden. A more recent variation, called results-based sequencing of support, would use the same joining of immediate and up-front commitment of future support and add to that the requirement that the future support would be released only if and when specific targets, chosen by the recipient country itself, are achieved.

A fifth category comprises various options for modernizing the existing instruments for bilateral or multilateral lending so as to be more responsive to recipient country requirements. For example, lending in local currencies rather than in dollars would reduce the difficulties that some countries experience in managing their currency exchange risks. Greater flexibility in how guarantees are provided—and on what terms—is a high priority for some countries. Also, there is a strong view in some quarters that some of the multilaterals should "use their balance sheet" more aggressively in the sense of deploying their assets more actively to support their mission, rather than being overly conservative in how much lending and grant making they do.

Other categories cover further debt relief beyond the Highly Indebted Poor Countries (HIPC) initiative or full implementation of the G-8 Gleneagles commitments, the provision of risk insurance for natural disasters and other problems (for example, collapses in crop prices), and more strategic management of voluntary giving (the tsunami response highlighted the need for this). Also, remittances—payments from migrants back to their home countries—have recently been more clearly appreciated for the hugely important source of financial flows into developing countries that they truly are. Total remittances worldwide now exceed $126 billion per year and for some countries are one of their largest sources of foreign exchange, or *the* largest.

Beyond all these options, there are a host of others that sit more squarely—or entirely—in the private sector alone. The vast and multifaceted engine of private sector investing, both through markets and through direct private arrangements, has a towering presence in the development process as noted above, and questions about how to draw on and harness that dynamism are highly prominent now. One proposal, called Global Development Bonds, is described in a later section.

Other options within the private sector span the spectrum from microsize firms to the slightly larger enterprises at the small and medium-size level and on into larger ventures. At the micro end, microcredit is now a burgeoning business and crowded field, with many new actors and initiatives.

Microcredit's close cousin, microenterprise development, combines the finance of microcredit with the hands-on technical assistance and training of business development programs. Firms that grow beyond that, and cross into the small end of small and medium-size enterprise, enter a danger zone where the relatively larger infusion of capital they need to thrive is either extremely difficult for them to obtain or comes at a cost so high to them that they are at risk of being crushed by daunting repayment obligations. Both these areas—microenterprise development and the next step up from it—have needs that no one has figured out yet how to meet on a large scale, fully and sustainably.

For still larger firms, and for other forms of larger investments (for example, project finance for infrastructure improvements), the key challenge is to reduce the risks to investors as much as possible in each specific country situation. Only then will they provide more support in that setting, with more potential benefits for development.

That risk reduction needs to begin with ensuring that the country's "investment climate"—that is, the full gamut or policies and practices that determine its macroeconomic and microeconomic policies, legal and judicial systems, and so on—is as solid as possible, given that investor confidence is everything. Helping countries strengthen their investment climate is a core part of the mandate of the international financial institutions such as the World Bank.

In addition, risk reduction also requires the reduction of high information costs. An investor in New York who is not confident of knowing all the ins and outs of a prospective investment halfway around the world in Indonesia has to assign a much higher risk rating to that undertaking than she would otherwise or than the investment itself, fairly and fully assessed, might warrant. Often that higher rating can be fatal to whether a worthwhile investment goes ahead or not. Markets find ways of lowering information costs where there are good returns to be had, but history is replete with cases where bold steps by early movers were needed to get progress started. Who would need to do what in this case—to jump-start the squeezing down of information costs—and what sorts of enticements would be needed to accelerate that process point toward other potential options for innovative financing? The Global Development Bonds concept outlined below could be developed further in that direction.

## What to Make of It All

Making sense of this heterogeneous multitude of proposals—to understand them better and how they relate to one another—is no simple matter. A logical place to begin is with the options' objectives—that is, what they are aiming to achieve. This is a natural extension of the broader question, noted above, of why search at all for new approaches.

For virtually all the options here, the underlying objective has two elements: a specific problem to be fixed, such as a disease or the effects of natural disasters for uninsured parties, and a financing "opportunity," such as debt to be repaid (in the case of the polio debt buydowns) or the terms of lending (in the case of the local currency lending option). In some options, the originating problem to be fixed is more salient, as in the case of market interventions for key medicines. In others, the financing opportunity seems to have more weight, as in the case of debt relief.

Either way, problems and opportunities should drive decisions about which options to pursue, rather than vice versa—that is, rather than starting with interesting "solutions" and then looking for problems to apply them to. Leading from problems to solutions seems, in fact, to be what the options so far have done, although not entirely. One exception may be electronic-billing-based fundraising, which is a proposal to enable householders in developed countries, on a voluntary basis, to have their monthly electricity, water, or other utility payments automatically rounded up and the "remainder change" then sent to programs in developing countries. Whatever appeal this idea may have—and preliminary estimates suggest it could raise a few billion dollars a year if done on a global scale—it is unlikely to gain much traction without a compelling link to a tangible problem to be solved, such as malaria control.

Other insights on the options can be gleaned from looking at them as a group from the perspective of the sources and destinations of the financial flows they would generate—that is, where the funds would come from and where they would go. A table like the one shown in box 7-2 can help in this regard. A more detailed definition of sources and destinations as in box 7-3, with distinctions too among flows (1) within a developing country and (2) from outside, may be needed for some applications.

One insight that emerges from reflecting on the possibilities from this viewpoint is that policymakers seeking the best and most efficient strategies for promoting development are probably not spending enough time thinking about this matrix and where their optimal choices are. The tendency—in government, business, civil society, philanthropies, and donors—to focus mostly on one's own backyard, and not internalize creatively the many ways of working with others and through their backyards, is always difficult to overcome. Put another way, most thinking today, in the daily work of translating objectives to action, is confined too much to the diagonal entries in box 7-2 (for example, from public sector to itself, from financial sector to itself). Too little exploration is done, in the heat of the battle to get things working, of the off-diagonal cells, where one partner links up with another.

Related to this point is another: many of the most interesting options involve combinations of multiple actors, particularly public-private partnerships of diverse kinds. An example—"results-based sequences of loans and grants"—is discussed below.

Ultimately, the best way from the perspective of choosing among options, as noted above, is to ask how they compare in the benefits they would yield in relation to the costs of adopting them. The public as well as the private benefits and costs of the options would need to be carefully considered in that analysis, along with what would happen if no action is taken. The feasibility—institutionally and politically—of the options would also need to be assessed, as would the time they would take to be effective and the supporting actions, if any, that would be required.

The importance of this benefit/cost perspective is illustrated by a comparison of two options currently attracting attention: the Advance Purchase Commitment and the Targeted Exclusions from Patent Rights for Key Medicines. They have very different footprints in their benefits and costs.

In an Advance Purchase Commitment, a group of funders (public, private, or a mix) would commit to provide financing—say, $3 billion—that would

BOX 7-2

## Organizing the Options Where Funds Come from and Go To

| | *Public sector* | *Financial sector* | *Corporate sector* | *Small, medium-size, and micro-enterprise* | *Civil society* | *Donor programs* | *Households* |
|---|---|---|---|---|---|---|---|
| *Public sector* | Developing countries' own development programs | Government support to financial and corporate institutions during financial or economic crises | | Government-supported local development banks | Government programs administered or monitored by civil society organizations | Fee-based services (for example, technical assistance) provided by international agencies | Developing countries' own development programs |
| *Financial sector* | International banks take financial positions in developing country projects and firms. Ideas for facilitating more lending include Global Development Bonds. | | | Local bank lending for microcredit and SME development | Philanthropic or corporate social responsibility initiatives | Joint ventures (for example, with the International Finance Corporation) | Home loans |
| *Corporate sector* | Tax payments and license fees | Commercial loans | Foreign Direct Investment (FDI) | Subcontracting | | | Wages paid to employees |
| *Small, medium-size, and micro-enterprise* | | Local bank lending for microcredit and SME development | Franchising | Start-up support—from families and sweat equity | SME firms' support to local community organizations | NGO support to SMEs (for example, Technoserve) | |

| | *Public sector* | *Financial sector* | *Corporate sector* | *Small, medium-size, and micro-enterprise* | *Civil society* | *Donor programs* | *Households* |
|---|---|---|---|---|---|---|---|
| *Civil society* | Debt buydowns (for example, Rotarians on polio) | Church groups form credit unions | Growers' collectives negotiate with corporates | NGO programs | | | |
| *The "official donors"* | Aid projects, as traditionally done for more than fifty years | IFI assistance for strengthening a country's financial sector | IFI programs with private sector partners (as in the IFC and its equivalents in other IFIs) | | Donor programs administered or monitored by civil society organizations | Donor co-financing and other partnerships | Relief programs (for example, after natural disasters) |
| *Philanthropic sector* | Debt buydowns (for example, Gates on polio) | International Finance Facility | | Foundations' programs | | | |
| *Remittances* | Community improvement programs | Transmittal fees | Cross-border enterprises and investing by diasporas | | Community improvement programs | | Migrant workers send money home |

Note: SME = small and medium-size enterprises; FDI = foreign direct investment; NGO = nongovernmental organization; IFI = international financial institution; IFC = International Finance Corporation.

BOX 7-3

## The Sources and Destinations of Financing in More Detail

*Public sector:* The various components of developing country governments (for example, as sovereign, as national agencies such as a ministry of health, as subnational entities, or as public enterprises; and through both on-budget or off-budget flows). Public sector support from outside the country appears under "official donors" support below.

*Financial sector:* Banks and other financial institutions, pension and insurance entities, other institutional investors, and investment firms including private equity and venture capital groups. The resulting flows, both domestic and from global capital markets, encompass both debt and equity finance.

*Corporate sector:* Local firms and multinationals (for example, *Fortune* 100 companies). Includes both their direct investment in plants and equipment and their portfolio investment.

*Small enterprises, medium-size enterprises, and microenterprises:* Though some of these firms are big enough to get capital from the markets, many are so small that they have to rely only on start-up sweat equity. Others, in between these extremes, are at risk of dying in the no-man's-land of capital starvation.

*Civil society:* Nongovernmental organizations, faith-based organizations, labor groups, and the like. Both local and international.

*"Official donors":* The bilaterals (for example, the Europeans, the United States, Japan, and others through their aid programs and sometimes through other channels too, such as their export-import banks, and foreign and military assistance). Also, the multilaterals (the international financial institutions, including the International Monetary Fund, the World Bank, the regional and subregional development banks), the UN agencies, and others, including the European Union.

*Philanthropic sector:* Private foundations, corporate foundations, and voluntary giving.

*Remittances:* Flows across borders (for example, from migrants back to their home countries) and within countries (for example, from city workers back to their rural origins).

only be called upon if and when some crucial, agreed result is achieved—say, the successful development of an effective vaccine against malaria. The funders' binding commitment would be aimed at providing an incentive for more effort to develop the desired product—in this case, by the institutions that have the capability to do so, which are by and large the pharmaceutical companies (which otherwise have higher-reward, lower-risk options in research for products that sell well in developed countries). This idea is currently in fashion—but it is costly. The more than $3 billion price tag may cause sticker shock among the possible funders, and it is not clear that public sources could summon sufficient political will to play their necessary role.

In the Targeted Exclusions from Patent Rights for Key Medicines option, pharmaceutical companies would give up patent protection for selected vital drugs that have no market in the poorest countries. Certain heart medicines, for example, are badly needed everywhere but do not reach very-low-income countries because of their high cost. Under the Targeted Exclusions idea, the patent holder would allow countries with a per capita income below, say, $1,000 a year to produce the drug locally without paying patent royalties. Cheaper generics would then be available in those countries. Proponents argue that this would not hurt the pharmaceutical companies, because they could never sell these particular medicines in such poor countries. They also say that the usual fears about reverse flows of pills produced cheaply in developing countries that would be shipped back to rich country markets would be unfounded in this case, because consumers in the developed world would never accept generics from the least-developed world for such a sensitive health need.

This intervention costs little or nothing, unlike the $3 billion and more for an Advance Purchase Commitment for a vaccine. But the concept's feasibility, political and otherwise, seems doubtful. Concerns that this initiative would weaken efforts worldwide to strengthen intellectual property rights would spark sharp opposition from those who have large stakes in that agenda. Indeed, precisely for that reason, the Targeted Exclusions from Patent Rights idea has gone nowhere since it first was suggested a few years ago.

Different problems may require different solutions, obviously. What is appropriate to stimulate development of a vaccine for malaria may be very different from what is right for an existing heart medicine. Some problems too are clearly more significant than others; malaria is a major killer worldwide, whereas heart disease, though a major concern, affects far fewer people.

Other basic questions need to be pursued as well. In particular, are there *gaps* that should be explored? Similarly, are there additional lessons from looking at the whole array together that have not been obvious so far, or at least have not been recognized and acted upon fully to date, because many of the options were developed in isolation from one another?

Although these and other questions deserve further investigation, there is another more important point. Thinking about how the options stack up against one another may in the end be less helpful than identifying those that should be further examined and assessed and then ensuring that they get this attention. In other words, conducting a beauty contest among them is less important than certifying which can fly and which cannot. There is a reason why this observation is especially pertinent in this case. Many different options are needed in practice, because specific situations with various requirements will be best served by different financing strategies, and because no single option will be so effective that there will not be a need for many.

The options that, from that standpoint, should be examined and assessed in more detail are those that appear to have potential but have not been already studied sufficiently or completely and correctly. By these criteria, many options are not a priority now for further examination—short of just plain trying them out and assessing what happens. The IFF and global taxation of air travel, for instance, have been much written about already, and the fact that they have not found sufficient backing thus far to be close to broad adoption may be signal enough that the political obstacles may be daunting and that any other unanswered questions about them are moot.

Winnowing down, in this way, the full list of options to just those that most deserve attention now, this analysis found several of particular interest. The remainder of the chapter discusses three of them, leaving others for future work.

## Results-Based Sequencing of Loans and Grants

As noted above, the "results-based sequencing of loans and grants" option is essentially an extended and broadened form of the "debt buydowns" employed successfully in the polio eradication campaign. In that case, a coalition with prominent grant funding from the Rotarians and the Bill and Melinda Gates Foundation helped countries pay off (hence "buy down") debt from loans from the World Bank that were needed by those countries to mount intensive efforts to wipe out polio.

The extended or broadened form combines the original concept with results-based (that is, output-based) conditioning of support on performance.

Here is how it works. A developing country's government and an external funder together work out a program of support, under which the government undertakes to reach certain goals by specified dates (for example, improve antimalaria programs and achieve a particular reduction in malaria deaths). The external funder agrees to support the work through either a loan (for example, from the World Bank) or a grant (for example, from a bilateral donor or a philanthropic institution). So far, this is nothing new, but here comes the difference.

A third party—most likely another grant financier but conceivably a lender—is part of the deal from the outset, committing to provide additional support when and only when the specified targets have been attained. The additional funding can be thought of as supporting the next phase of the work or ensuring the sustainability of the program or, as was the case in the polio eradication campaign, providing funds to pay off a part or all of the initial loan, if there was one.

All three parties gain from this scheme. The country gets the money up front that is needed to do the work and then has the assurance of more to follow if the work is properly completed. Its government gets other benefits as well, including possibly the prospect of paying off some debt, always a popular move with voters. The initial external funder has greater prospects of seeing its support result in the desired outcomes. And the third-party financier can tell its overseers that its money will be released only when the results it is intended to support have already been achieved. Also, if it puts the money aside at the start of the whole endeavor, the value of that capital grows over time up to the point (for example, five years later) when it is drawn down.

There can also be benefits in the form of increased harmonization among donors, to the degree that the linking together of aid flows in results-based sequences results in closer partnership, with the country, in coordinating what programs are supported and how. But this harmonization aspect is also one of the challenges that must be solved to make this sequencing option successful and suitable for scaling up, because donors have thus far found that aligning themselves together in their development work is far from an easy undertaking.

A second challenge is getting grant financiers on board with sufficient funds to achieve significant impact. Despite the early examples set by the Rotarians and the Gates Foundation, the foundation world has been slow to follow. Bilateral donors, especially in Europe, have not yet shown much interest but should, because they would gain a lot in terms of the objectives they are seeking in their assistance programs. Today, their traditional flows are having mixed results, with less leveraged effectiveness than could be achieved through results-based sequencing of aid. With so many donors now calling so strongly for more of a focus on results, there has never been a better time to pursue this option.

## Global Development Bonds

Private financial flows to developing countries have exceeded public flows since the end of the 1980s, although debt and equity figures have been volatile, trending downward at times since the late 1990s, and focused on selected regions. But private foreign investment in developing countries could be much larger still were it not for various impediments, especially the risks involved.

Mitigation of investment risks of various kinds is now regular practice in developed countries, using many standard tools involving guarantees, insurance, securitization, tranching, overcollateralization, and so on. But risk mitigation instruments for investments in developing countries, despite various offerings from international institutions, local entities, and the markets, have remained extremely limited. As a result, developing countries, projects, and companies perceived to be high risk are largely unable to reach the higher credit ratings where more investors could participate and where investment terms would be significantly more favorable for them.

Lessening that constraint is the idea behind a concept called Global Development Bonds (GDBs), which would seek to achieve greater risk mitigation for developing country investments through thoughtful application, with adaptation where needed, of some of the same financial engineering techniques that have proven effective in the developed world.

Those thinking seriously about GDBs include people with considerable financial market experience in the private sector and others versed in the development and political aspects of the issues. Term sheets and organizational structures have been prepared, laying out how the concept would work. The result, GDB proponents feel, could provide a boost to development in the same way as the municipal bond market provides for states and localities in the United States—though on a smaller scale.

As a "private-to-private" option, meaning that funds flow from the private sector (probably, mainly from developed countries) and go to private sector projects and firms in developing countries, GDBs would be free of some of the limitations that hamper the traditional aid programs from the public sector and the official international development institutions. They would, in essence, do what the World Bank does—packaging low-credit-rating investments (developing country projects) in ways that result in a higher-rated aggregate (the World Bank is rated AAA) that can borrow on favorable terms and pass on the savings to poorer clients. But unlike the World Bank, GDBs would operate entirely through private markets. Both channels—private-to-private and public and official initiatives—have strengths and weaknesses, so there are advantages to a strategy that draws on both and sees them as complementing each other.

The backstopping enhancements that make GDBs viable need to be significant enough to make a difference. Though creative financial engineering in the private sector can cover part of that distance, some backing through public action may also be required as the necessary legal and financial authorities are being established to launch GDBs. Varying degrees of public backing could be considered. In the U.S. context, the least demanding might be to enable the federal government's Overseas Private Investment Corporation to strengthen its support. Other larger steps could include granting of authority to invest, to a small and hard-limited extent, in a joint private-public entity that would help re-guarantee GDBs and the authorization of slightly more expanded support through special-purpose vehicles or government-sponsored entities.

The specific risks that would be covered could also be variously defined. Risks connected with currency fluctuations, possible political changes in countries, policy reversals, regulatory shifts, and social pressures pose differing challenges for which existing risk mitigation mechanisms offer extensive experience. GDBs would not cover another category of risks—commercial risks—which capture the underlying uncertainties about the business venture itself.

The developers of the GDB idea reasonably observe that even a modest start could significantly increase financial flows to developing country investments. Compared with the roughly $70 billion in official aid to developing countries annually, 270 times that amount—about $19 trillion—is invested in U.S. securities markets. If only a few tenths of a percent of that private capital shifted to investments in developing countries, the increase in flows into those countries could dwarf the flows from aid. Risk mitigation that enabled the large institutional investors to join in would also have a potentially large impact. U.S. pension funds alone totaled $7.8 trillion in 2004; U.S. life insurance company assets were $4.2 trillion.

The developers are aware that their explorations will be regarded in some quarters as politically impossible. But at a time when other approaches to fighting global poverty—such as the current U.S. administration's Millennium Challenge Corporation—are finding their way, GDBs offer an option that has the political attraction of being squarely a private sector–led initiative and requiring no budget allocations, an important consideration at a time when the budgetary climate has rarely been worse.

As the developers also note, every other change in the past—including the special provisions for municipal bonds—was once viewed as utterly unimaginable. Naysayers are inevitable—but they are not always right.

Much more needs to be investigated before it will be clear whether GDBs are a promising option and, if so, what their particulars should be. Specialists are now developing term sheets and flowcharts and testing the political waters. Time will tell where this leads.

## Investing in Grassroots Business Organizations

At the opposite extreme from the huge macro-level high visibility of GDBs is the "bottom-of-the-pyramid" world of microfinance, microenterprise development, and social entrepreneurship. Much has been written about this vibrant universe of small-can-make-big ideas that are private sector–based in the most elemental sense of building up from nothing.

Microfinance per se—that is, providing cash without also providing business advice, training, technical assistance, and the like—has become a crowded field. Further testing and drawing of lessons from various approaches would clearly be useful, not least because faster expansion will create more opportunities sooner for the bottom rungs on the economic ladder. More evidence will also help on the differing challenges across regions, countries, industries and sectors, and cultural groups. Also on firm size, there is a world of difference between the tiniest of the "micro" category and the larger heft of the next category up (called, confusingly, "small") and the still bigger wingspan of "medium," which is still well below that of "large" enterprises. Special problems of firms caught in "dead spots" in this size spectrum—having grown out of a backyard venture but not yet become big enough to have access to the larger capital they need to grow further—are being better documented now.

Related to this debate, a tidbit from the history of providing enterprise credit is revealing. For decades of the twentieth century, efforts to provide finance to emerging firms failed one after another. Then, just in the past few years, a flowering of new attempts has had impressively successful results. Why the difference? The earlier efforts were mostly dominated by the public sector: government-run development finance institutions. Ineffective management, poor loan recovery rates, and high costs killed them. The new breed is entirely private sector led—both from above (the Citigroup example mentioned above) and from the country level (Unibanco)—and they have found robust ways to keep costs down and repayments up.

Microenterprise development—which provides business advice and more, in addition to finance—remains less charted terrain. Though many entrants are exploring the possibilities on a limited scale, it is not yet clear that they can be scaled up sustainably to levels that would make an appreciable dent in poverty. The costs and complexities of providing business advice, technical assistance, and training are much more daunting than simply providing money. But that hands-on support may be more important. Many firms, once they get above the very small, need major management strengthening as much as or more than money. (For example, a firm with an accounting problem cannot go on having the founder's untrained brother be the bookkeeper.) Cracking this problem—of how to support microenterprise development on a larger-scale basis—may be one of the preeminent challenges where private sector know-how and creativity are most needed.

One effort that is taking a promising stab at that is the Strengthening Grassroots Businesses Initiative (SGBI) spearheaded by Harold Rosen of the World Bank Group's International Finance Corporation. In their lexicon, grassroots business organizations are socially driven ventures, whether for-profit or not-for-profit, that reach out to those at the "base of the pyramid" as partners, suppliers, consumers, and beneficiaries. These businesses provide income, employment, and training for disadvantaged people, bridging the gap to the global marketplace.

SGBI aims to have a catalytic impact in this emerging sector, building partnerships with like-minded groups and leveraging its own resources, networks, and position within an international institution. It provides a package of funding and technical assistance to grassroots businesses, helping them expand their impact and creating opportunities for replication and scaling up. Complementing and building on this on-the-ground work, SGBI also supports intermediaries and associations serving multiple grassroots businesses, and it facilitates the sharing of experience and lessons learned with clients and partners.

With each qualifying business, SGBI follows a three-step approach. First, a pragmatic diagnosis of the business's operations identifies obstacles to growth and opportunities for improvements, taking into account its priority needs and possibilities to bring in partners to assist in capacity building and funding. Second, an action plan is agreed on with the business's leadership team, detailing operating, financial, and social performance targets and key milestones needed to reach those targets. And third, a combination of technical assistance and patient capital (for example, long-term, low-interest loans) is implemented, with funding provided as and when milestones in the action plan are met. The technical assistance is delivered through local providers as much as possible, with backstopping from resident International Finance Corporation staff.

An example is Honey Care in Kenya, an enterprise established expressly to increase the incomes of rural farmers. To date, Honey Care has doubled the income of more than 2,500 small-scale farmers through its "Money for Honey" program, which trains them in commercial beekeeping and then buys their honey at a guaranteed price. Honey Care then packages and sells the honey, which is of very high quality. SGBI is working to provide technical assistance and patient capital to Honey Care to further scale up its Kenyan operations and replicate its model in neighboring Tanzania (and potentially elsewhere).

SGBI's work with intermediaries and associations includes both financial and nonfinancial support as well—for example, by helping microfinance institutions broaden their reach and promoting the establishment or expansion of marketing centers for grassroots business products. As SGBI strengthens these one-tier-up intermediaries and associations, it will be able to expand its own reach—which is part of its business model too—moving, in effect, from a retail to a wholesale scale.

## Conclusions

If the growing list of ideas and proposals for innovative approaches to financing is analyzed using frameworks like box 7-2 and concepts such as cost-benefit assessment incorporating political and other feasibility considerations, will we learn more than we know now? Will the current options become easier to understand and prioritize in terms of which deserve more research or immediate action and which appear less promising? Will new options come to light and be easier to spot and develop early on? Though this chapter merely scratches the surface of these questions, initial indications are encouraging.

The three examples described above—results-based sequencing of loans and grants, global development bonds, and investing in grassroots business organizations—demonstrate some of the vast variety of proposals that are emerging. They also reflect several more general points noted at the outset. All have potential, but verifying that potential would require testing them in practice and assessing their feasibility and impacts carefully. Furthermore, even if successful, none would obviate the need for other efforts as well, including existing initiatives and instruments and continued search for better ones. There is no silver bullet in this batch; each would help on some problems but would not solve them all.

Another hypothesis suggested by the range of current options is that there has been an imbalance of attention thus far, with much focus on the public sector together with "official donors" and too little on options rooted in private sector activity. Yet the prospects for significant impact in accelerating development and reducing poverty may well be the reverse. The public and "official donor" sector options may have more limited impact than has been generally supposed, either because they will involve much smaller capital flows or will have difficulty getting widely adopted and implemented. The experience with the IFF, now funded by far fewer donor countries than had been hoped for originally, is an example. Conversely, the private sector options, with huge financial and organizational resources behind them, may have greater possible impact than they have been given credit for in the past.

Another related—but separate—hypothesis is that the conventional reasons sometimes given for dismissing private sector options may not be as compelling as was sometimes believed previously. The notion that market players—from the biggest institutional investors and venture capitalists down to the tiniest mutual fund accounts—have no interest in contributing to helping global development has been overturned by growing evidence that many want, at least with a small portion of their assets, to "not only continue doing well financially but also doing some good developmentally." And a small portion of a very, very large capital pool is still something more than small change.

Also, the notion that markets cannot or should not get enhancements backed by public sector commitments has begun to be questioned. Unlike some theorists opining from a distance, people who really know the markets from practical experience are pointing out that if the usual objections sometimes made to promising new ideas were followed to their limit, a major part of public policy accumulated over literally hundreds of years of public choices by voters and leaders would be ignored entirely.

A further general point underscored here is that the quest for innovative financing options needs to be properly and compellingly rooted in the overall objective of reducing poverty. This may seem rather obvious. But there is always the risk that fascination with instruments will weaken focus on the ultimate objectives that the instruments are intended to serve. The current "gold rush" for new financing ideas should not detract from appreciation of the need, in each developing country situation, to start first with a careful analysis of what the particular problems are in that society's fight to reduce poverty and then proceed to reasoned development of the appropriate solutions for each context.

No less important, practitioners and policymakers must remember that a new instrument, even if successful, may not necessarily have a large impact. Take, again, the microfinance example. Some players engaged in new approaches to expanding microfinance options believe that successful scaling up could provide a significant boost to development. Others feel that success, though an enormous help to some, would still have only a modest impact. Similar uncertainties surround expectations of what many other new interventions would yield. Efforts are planned now to reexamine the available evidence on these considerations and to develop better estimates that, however rough, could at least be of some use in deliberating which options should be explored.

## Reference

World Bank. 2005. *Global Development Finance: Mobilizing Finance and Managing Vulnerability.* Washington, D.C.

# 8

## 2 + 2 = 5: *A Pragmatic View of Partnerships between Official Donors and Multinational Corporations*

LARRY COOLEY

POLITICAL AND ECONOMIC developments during the past two decades have changed the level, composition, and destination of private investment and foreign aid flowing into developing countries and transition economies. Private flows (including remittances) and public funding of development projects have both risen during this period, but private flows have increased much more rapidly—now constituting more than 80 percent of funds moving from the United States into developing and transition countries (as compared with less than 30 percent in the 1970s).

Beginning with a focus on commercial agriculture in the 1960s, followed, successively, by attention to macroeconomic reform, structural adjustment, small enterprise credit, microenterprise, an enabling environment, business services, trade promotion, and competitiveness, official donors have long been concerned with publicly funded efforts to stimulate the private sector, often linked to broader strategies for poverty reduction. Since around 2000, multinational corporations have increasingly emerged as active development partners—not simply as indirect beneficiaries—providing financial resources, expertise, and other forms of support for these development efforts. Motivated by corporate social responsibility and by direct commercial incentives,

Larry Cooley is the founder and president of Management Systems International (MSI). He has also served as an adviser to cabinet- and sub-cabinet-level officials in the U.S. Departments of State, Interior, Agriculture, and Health and Human Services and the Small Business Administration; as a frequent consultant at the United Nations and the World Bank; and as adviser to senior officials in eight foreign countries.

corporations have entered into a number of different types of partnership with official donors.

This chapter compares methods employed by donors to foster private sector growth with a particular emphasis on public-private partnerships. It begins with a brief review of the history of public-private partnerships, describes some of the objectives and experiences of key public and private sector players, provides analysis of the ten unresolved issues surrounding public-private approaches, and provides recommendations for the future.

## A Brief History of Public-Private Partnerships

The United Nations defines the private sector as having four components: multinational corporations (MNCs), small and medium-size enterprises (SMEs), national large-scale enterprises (LSEs), and microenterprises. Donor programs have traditionally focused their efforts on the latter three categories of enterprises, in part because donors tended to view the private sector as a beneficiary of their programs rather than as a partner.

Over time, private sector development specialists have become a distinct category of development professional, taking their place beside development economists in discussions of how best to promote broad-based economic growth. Some donors, like the U.S. Agency for International Development (USAID), initially created a unique bureau to handle this new focus on private sector development (PSD).

In the 1980s many PSD programs focused on macroeconomic policy and SME credit. Beginning in about 1990, PSD programming evolved to include a range of efforts aimed at improving the business climate. Also in this second phase, trade capacity building and microenterprise creation were introduced as means to stimulate both PSD and poverty alleviation.

In a third phase, donors began to embed PSD approaches and incentives into a wide range of public sector initiatives (for example, health, family planning, and social marketing). During this phase, many donors, USAID included, eliminated the separate private enterprise bureaus they had created, arguing that it was preferable to mainstream PSD approaches into all relevant sectors and bureaus.

Many donors continue to operate first-, second-, and third-phase programs intended to promote the private sector by channeling public funds to government agencies and other publicly funded projects. Such programs include providing technical assistance, training, and other forms of support to policy and regulatory agencies; underwriting or capitalizing lending and venture capital activities; and subsidizing the provision of business and trade services for small and incipient enterprises. Among the leading official donors providing such programs are USAID, the World Bank Group, the United Nations Development Program (UNDP), and the bilateral aid programs of the United Kingdom (Department for International Development, or DFID), Germany (German Agency for Technical Cooperation, or GTZ), and Denmark (Danish International Development Agency, or Danida). A recent publication from the Organization for Economic Cooperation and Development—*Accelerating Pro-Poor Growth through Support for Private Sector Development*—extends this discussion with particular emphasis on best practices. Increasingly, these best practices emphasize structural and policy solutions that strengthen rather than substitute for normal commercial markets.

A fourth phase of donor programming—working with the corporate sector (MNCs and large local firms) as full partners in meeting economic and social needs in developing countries—began to gain momentum in the late 1990s. Building on the corporate social responsibility (CSR) movement in developed countries, these fourth-phase programs seek to leverage the skills and resources of corporations as benefactors as well as beneficiaries of the development process.

## Public-Private Partnerships and Alliances

The term "partnership" lacks consistent definition in the international development community. A partnership is generally understood to entail a voluntary pairing of two or more entities working together to achieve a result beneficial to each party. Normally, the term implies a sharing of risks and rewards, and it frequently connotes relative power symmetry. Within the international development community, other groups often referred to as "partners" include host country counterpart organizations, fee-for-service intermediaries, and program beneficiaries.

This definitional confusion is compounded with respect to public-private partnerships (PPPs) given the unusually wide array of motives and commitments of the parties involved. One way to distinguish among such partnerships is by looking at them in terms of the respective roles and responsibilities of the various parties. For example, the term "PPP" is frequently used to refer to the government practice of contracting out the provision of public services (for example, water, health care, electricity, garbage collection) and to the relationship between official donors and nongovernmental organizations (NGOs), even when the official donor pays all direct and indirect costs associated with the projects being carried out. To clarify this, some have begun to use the terms "implementing partner" and "resource partner" to distinguish partner roles, notwithstanding the fact that the same organization can often play both roles in a given partnership.

A second way to distinguish among categories of PPPs focuses on the depth and durability of the relationships among the parties. James Austin, in his book *The Collaboration Challenge* (Austin 2000), notes that collaborations (partnerships) move from traditional philanthropy toward strategic alliances along a collaboration continuum. Beginning with the *philanthropic stage*, typified by corporate contributions to worthy organizations and causes, collaborations often evolve to a *transactional* stage, at which resources are exchanged through specific activities to advance the organizations' respective agendas, and sometimes eventually advance to the *integrative stage* in which the collaboration is highly integrated with shared activities central to both parties' strategic objectives.

Two more recent publications—*Corporate Social Opportunity!* by David Grayson and Adrian Hodges (2004) and *Profits with Principles: Seven Strategies for Delivering Value with Values* by Ira Jackson and Jane Nelson (2004)—provide somewhat different and equally valuable lenses through which to view the nature and evolution of partnerships. Jackson and Nelson, for example, distinguish "one-way giving" from "strategic partnership" with respect to philosophy, methods, purpose, decisionmakers, recipients, reach, impact, employee involvement, relationship management, and nexus with core competencies.

A third way to categorize PPPs is in terms of the types of projects they carry out. In the international development arena, useful distinctions can be drawn between partnerships to promote private sector development, partnerships to promote standards, partnerships to govern transnational issues, and partnerships to utilize the skills and resources of the private sector to solve public problems. Examples of such partnerships, respectively, are supply chain development, certified products, global compacts, and provision of social services to underserved populations.

## A Widening Range of Actors and Approaches

The following paragraphs describe the most typical approaches to PPPs currently being taken by private corporations and international donors. Three corporations—Chevron, Starbucks, and Nike—and six major donors are profiled as a way of giving an overview of current practices and highlighting contrasting approaches.

### *Private Sector Approaches to PPPs*

As suggested above, there are many reasons why MNCs engage in public–private alliances and CSR, including gaining access to new markets, maintaining a "social license to operate" in key countries, helping to raise employee morale, responding to consumer or stockholder pressure, strengthening supply chains, and hedging risks. Rarely is pure philanthropy the motivation. By way of illustration, the following paragraphs describe the approaches taken by three MNCs well known for their creative use of PPPs and their commitment to CSR.

*Chevron.* As an energy company, Chevron operates and extracts resources in some of the poorest and least stable parts of the world. For reasons of risk management, it is imperative for the company to maintain a productive and healthy work force, a positive public image, and a supportive enabling environment in these countries. Internationally, the company is also anxious to cultivate a reputation as a good corporate citizen. With these objectives in mind, its three broad goals, as outlined in its *2003 Corporate Social Responsibility Report*, are encouraging economic and social progress, building the capacity of governments (through increased transparency in accounting for oil and gas operations), and reducing the negative environmental effects of energy development and use. One particularly innovative partnership, the $20 million Angola Partnership Initiative with USAID, is a coequal and jointly managed partnership that supports agricultural development, funding of SMEs (for example, the establishment of the country's first microcredit bank), a Center for Enterprise Development, and various HIV/AIDS programs. Chevron also maintains an active alliance with UNDP in Angola.

*Starbucks.* Starbucks's public–private partnerships stress social and environmental stewardship, and its 2004 CSR theme was "striking a balance" between fiscal responsibility and enhancing the lives of those affected by the coffee business. Many of its CSR activities make use of the firm's considerable buying power and supply chain to provide cash incentives and market access for producers that comply with global environmental or social benchmarks. They also help producers reach these standards. For example, Starbucks opened a Farmer Support Center in Costa Rica in 2004 that enables local coffee farmers to interact with coffee-growing experts on quality and sustainability practices and linked its sourcing to these same standards. Starbucks also provided $1.5 million to its alliance with Conservation International (CI) and USAID to help expand CI's program, including enforcing a set of responsible coffee-buying principles. The firm's product marketing prominently features its socially and environmentally conscious policies and includes programs with a wide range of nonprofits, including CARE International, African Wildlife Foundation, and Mercy Corps. Some of these programs involve direct participation by Starbucks establishments, and all have a direct connection to coffee growing or to the well-being of coffee farmers, their families, and communities.

*Nike.* In response to criticism over some of its operating practices, Nike is actively focusing company attention on CSR and has a publicly stated goal of being the CSR leader of the twenty-first century. It believes that CSR is good for business (for example, builds supply chain excellence and deepens relationships with consumers) and discloses its supply base in an effort to show its ethical business practices. In addition, it has a set of partnerships in developing countries through the Nike Foundation, founded in 1994, to work in a limited set of countries on two of the United Nations' Millennium Development Goals—poverty alleviation and gender equality. Most projects focus on developing "safe spaces" where girls learn leadership skills and interact with trusted adults. In each country, the foundation works with selected partners to identify and develop projects, because it does not accept unsolicited proposals. The foundation's programs are funded by its annual target of 3 percent of the previous year's pretax income.

Of the many distinctions among different corporations' approaches to PPP, most noteworthy for the purposes of this chapter are the obvious differences among these companies in the primary audience to which their programs are addressed and the extent to which programs link to the companies' products and supply chain. Also critically important is the predisposition of some companies to generate programs and seek partners, while other companies seek to join the efforts of established donors, and still others to respond to solicitations from third parties.

### Donor Approaches to PPPs

Donor approaches to PPPs differ principally in whether and how the donor is prepared to form partnerships with specific companies, whether it focuses on policies or on transactions, and whether it sees itself as a facilitator, convener, implementer, financier, guarantor of good practices, or some combination of these roles. As the following brief descriptions illustrate, these differences hinge in some measure on the differing mandates of multilateral and bilateral donors and—in the case of bilateral donors—the link (if any) between international development and trade promotion.

***United Nations Development Program.*** UNDP plays a leadership role in the UN Global Compact, an interagency network (composed of UNDP, Office of the UN High Commissioner for Refugees, UN Environment Program, International Labor Organization, UN Industrial Development Organization, and UN Office on Drugs and Crime) launched operationally in July 2000 at the direct initiative of the UN secretary general. The Global Compact is a voluntary initiative that brings together the aforementioned UN agencies, labor, governments, businesses, and civil society to encourage companies around the world to be more socially responsible by following a set of ten universally recognized principles in the areas of human rights, labor rights, the environment, and anticorruption, with the aim of eventually mainstreaming them in companies' business practices. It relies on public accountability, transparency, and the newly perceived self-interest of companies to promote these ends, and it operates through a series of policy dialogues, country and regional networks, and projects. It conceives of itself as a platform on which initiatives should be launched and new partnerships should emerge.

Relationships with the business sector are carried out by UNDP's Division for Business Partnerships. UNDP currently has partnerships with more than twenty corporations across a broad range of sectors: SME development, democratic governance, information technology, HIV/AIDS, energy and environment, and promotion of Global Compact local networks. In these partnerships, UNDP prefers to serve as a broker and/or facilitator rather than as a direct funder or implementer of discrete projects so as to leverage its strengths (that is, as a promoter of dialogue amongst stakeholders, the convener, and an impartial third party). On rare occasions, it also serves as an implementing partner or a source of financial support for a specific initiative. In one example, UNDP worked with the Venezuelan government, Amnesty International, and Statoil in Venezuela to train judges and prosecutors on international human rights law.

UNDP also serves as a convener and facilitator for the Growing Sustainable Business initiative and the newly created Corporate Partnerships in Emergencies Program. In the first initiative, UNDP works with companies looking to invest in developing countries within their core business or value chain to create sustainable pro-poor solutions, while in the latter, it channels private sector contributions to areas of need after both natural and human-created disasters. Within the Bureau for Development Policy, the division for Public Private Partnerships for the Urban Environment supports local governments in their reform of business sectors responsible for the delivery of basic services.

*World Bank Group.* Business Partners for Development (BPD) was launched by the World Bank in 1998 to study, support, and promote deliberate trisectoral partnerships. (Trisectoral partnerships bring together public, private, and non-profit or NGO actors.) As an early innovator of PPPs, BPD sought to demonstrate that trisectoral partnerships could be beneficial arrangements for all partners, rather than just engaging the private sector in a philanthropic endeavor as had been customary until this point.

BPD used an investment of $38 million to carry out pilot projects in four sectors—water and sanitation, natural resources, global road safety, and youth development—in addition to further investments by the private sector, foundations, governments, and the World Bank to cover the operational costs of projects. Though each cluster had different projects and different private sector and foundation partners, the common thread running through all partnerships was their structure. A secretariat for each cluster supported project appraisal, analysis, and dissemination. Sponsors, which included private sector partners, foundations, governments, and the World Bank, supported projects' operational costs. A common Knowledge Resource Group supported all four clusters. All parties involved in a given project agreed upon one common vision, a mutually determined set of objectives and work plan, a set of grievance mechanisms to resolve disputes, and mechanisms for ongoing transparency and for monitoring and evaluation. BPD, which was created to last for three years (1998–2001), helped to set the stage for other multilateral and bilateral donors to follow with their own PPPs.

As the private sector arm of the World Bank Group, the International Finance Corporation (IFC) is the largest multilateral source of loan and equity support for projects in developing countries. In 2003 nearly $4 billion was spent on private sector projects in an effort to stimulate further private sector growth. To ensure participation by all parties, the IFC will not contribute more than 25 percent of the total project cost, with investments ranging from $1 million to $100 million. With no standard application procedure, the IFC continually solicits proposals from companies and entrepreneurs who have been unable to secure funding from alternative sources. The IFC also provides advice and technical assistance to governments in these countries focused on project financing and resource mobilization. It is obliged by its mission to ensure that projects attain high environmental and social standards and are responsive to the concerns of stakeholders and other interested parties.

*U.S. Agency for International Development.* A leading proponent of PPPs, USAID launched the Global Development Alliance (GDA) in 2001 as a new business model intended to engage new partners, leverage new resources, and fundamentally change USAID operating procedures. (USAID refers to its PPPs as public–private alliances, or PPAs; however, for the sake of consistency in this chapter, they are referred to as PPPs.) A small unit in Washington serves as the centralized contact point for outside partners, spearheads the revision of agency procedures, provides training and guidance materials for USAID staff, offers seed funding for selected partnerships, and maintains a comprehensive database on agency performance in implementing public–private partnerships. Partnerships are integrated into the plans and budgets of all bureaus and missions, and each partnership is managed by the operating unit most closely related to the partnership's sector or country of focus.

Unlike traditional USAID projects, GDA partnerships are intended to be the product of joint planning and shared risks and rewards between USAID and the resource partners with which it cooperates. In addition to technical support and market access, partners are expected to provide funding at least equal to that provided by USAID. These funds can be either commingled or administered in parallel with USAID funds. USAID recently commissioned AccountAbility and MSI to carry out a multicountry study of PPP governance aimed at documenting best practices and informing future action.

During its first three and a half years, the GDA initiative provided approximately $1 billion in USAID funding to support 290 alliances in 98 countries. Each dollar of USAID funding invested in these programs leveraged an average of more than $3 of funding from outside partners. Though the majority of PPPs were not health related, health-related PPPs received substantially more funding per project. Given the emphasis from the outset on mainstreaming, less than 10 percent of USAID funding for alliances came from funds administered by the GDA Secretariat, with the majority coming from the regular budgets of bureaus and missions.

Among other innovative USAID PPP programs is the Development Credit Authority, set up in 1999 to establish or extend the lending of funds for private sector investment in developing countries by providing partial credit guarantees to local commercial lenders. Since its inception, it has signed more than 100 loans, which have generated $855 million in new loans (a leverage ratio of 25:1 on every dollar spent).

***U.K. Department for International Development.*** In addition to its long-standing programs to promote private sector development in poor countries, DFID has undertaken to coordinate efforts across Whitehall focused on corporate social responsibility. Especially notable initiatives are the Ethical Trading

Initiative, an alliance of U.K. retail companies, NGOs, and trade unions that works to improve labor conditions in the country supply chains of its corporate members in observance of International Labor Organization conventions; and the Extractive Industries Transparency Initiative (EITI), which promotes openness regarding the payments by extractive industries to governments and government-linked entities and in the revenues of host governments from the sale of extractive products. EITI was initially piloted in Nigeria; then expanded to Ghana, Azerbaijan, and Kyrgyzstan; and now includes a total of nine countries. Other related DFID-supported CSR efforts include Just Pensions, Pro-Poor Investment Reporting, and support for the Fair Trade movement in the United Kingdom.

DFID earmarks funds for Business Partners for Development led by the World Bank (see the description above) and for related World Bank programs to enhance host country capacity to set up and administer voluntary frameworks and standards for corporate social responsibility. In addition, DFID funds projects fostering corporate social responsibility in several countries, mostly in Africa. For example, the Kenyan Business Partnerships Program, cofunded and run by the Kenya Federation of Employers, encourages and assists employers to incorporate social responsibility and ethical trading principles into their core businesses and to conduct social responsibility audits.

Although most DFID efforts occur at the policy level, the institution also funds transactions. "Challenge Funds" are divided into two main types—Business Linkage Challenge Funds (BLCFs) and Financial Deepening Challenge Funds (FDCFs). Nearly three-fourths of the BLCF projects are in Africa, with approximately half of these in South Africa. The private sector must apply for funds in bidding cycles that occur twice a year with fixed application deadlines; the grants sought range from £50,000 to £1 million. At least one partner must be registered in the United Kingdom and one partner must be registered in the targeted country. While small-size partnerships tend to be more commercially focused and justified in terms of job creation, larger corporations also seek funding for CSR projects not related to their core business functions. For the FDCF, bidders (that is, financial institutions) must cover at least 50 percent of project costs, and the project must increase access to commercially sustainable financial services for poor people or for businesses that employ poor people.

*German Agency for Technical Cooperation.* Within GTZ, the Center for Cooperation with the Private Sector has carried out PPPs on behalf of the

German Federal Ministry for Economic Cooperation and Development since 1999. For each partnership, the private partner—a German company—must pay for at least 50 percent of the costs. Projects are jointly planned and financed with participating German companies, and GTZ conceives of these programs as making it possible for participating German firms to benefit directly from the government-to-government relationships established through GTZ's technical cooperation programs. It is also GTZ's hope that the business-to-business links formed through the program will lead to long-term business linkages.

Total funding for the nearly 250 PPP projects completed to date is more than e161 million, with GTZ contributing e57.4 million, private partners contributing e77.3 million, and third parties contributing the remaining amount. (The number of project inquiries far exceeds the number of projects that GTZ is able and willing to fund. Projects last for one to three years, and more than half focus on economic reform in developing countries, with additional projects focusing on a host of sectors, the most popular being agriculture, the environment, and health. The most popular regions are Asia and Africa, with 112 and 82 projects, respectively.

GTZ perceives its role as helping to fund a substantial number of pilot projects, which are dropped if they prove ineffective and are expected to be ramped up (typically without GTZ funding) if they are successful. To receive funding, all projects must go beyond the scope of the company's core business and are supposed to have solid development and economic objectives. Like some other donors, but unlike USAID, GTZ plays the role of convener and partial financier, but it plays little further role during implementation. Thus, it looks for commercial partners that can contribute technology, capital, and expertise and that are willing to implement projects with good prospects for sustainability and for making a tangible contribution to the country in which they are implemented.

*Danish International Development Agency.* Danida conducts poverty alleviation and development work in sixteen countries. In its effort to strengthen the private sector and provide an attractive enabling environment in selected developing countries, it actively engages Danish businesses to serve as partners to local businesses. Within the Department for Business Cooperation and Technical Assistance, the Private Sector Development Program (PSDP) has been in operation since 1993. Danida conceives of its role as facilitator and cofinancier—it does not get involved in any part of project implementation. Danida has moved from assisting Danish companies by providing subsidies to schemes in which Danish companies can benefit only indirectly. Companies in either Denmark or in developing countries can contact either the PSDP or the Danish embassy in the target country to discuss partnerships.

Danida supported the recent establishment of a Corporate Social Responsibility contact group for representatives of the Foreign Ministry and Danish industry. The group seeks to serve as a locus for cooperative efforts to promote guidelines on CSR and human rights. Danida has in this regard been a very active supporter of the UN Norms on Transnational Corporations and a source of core funding for the Global Compact Secretariat overseen by UNDP. Danida explicitly integrates these considerations into its "business sector programs," currently operating in Vietnam and Ghana.

As a follow-up to the Johannesburg Summit, the Danish government launched a new Initiative for Public-Private Partnerships. Beginning in 2004, it earmarked DKK 100 million to support PPPs between Danida and Danish businesses, with the aim of strengthening social and economic development in Danida-assisted countries. The eligibility criteria for these projects emphasize additionality—that is, the activities being funded must be outside the core commercial activities of the Danish enterprises involved. These enterprises must also contribute a minimum of 50 percent of the project's funding.

## Ten Unresolved Issues

PPPs between multinational corporations and official donors are, without question, expanding dramatically in number, range of partners, and diversity. They are also becoming decidedly more "partner-like," thereby taking fuller advantage of the distinctive capacities and motives of each participant. There are, however, a number of unresolved issues that limit the effectiveness of these partnerships and that, if unresolved, are likely to result in increasing frustration and declining enthusiasm for such partnerships. Most notable among these unresolved issues are the following ten.

### *Misaligned Expectations*

In stark contrast to normal business partnerships, the objectives and motives of international donors and their private sector partners in PPPs are strikingly diverse and badly articulated. The rationale for working in partnership can include comparative advantage, burden sharing, and seeing the other party as a source of credibility or access. For donor agencies, additional motives include promoting support for their programs at home, fostering unsubsidized replication of successful programs, and enhancing benefit sustainability through the use of market incentives. Though some corporate motives link directly to product placement, supply chain protection, or consumer pressure, many times programs and motives are more indirect. There is substantial evidence that failure to fully understand the objectives of the other party greatly complicates the governance of PPPs. Other areas of frequent misunderstanding concern the pace and locus of decisionmaking and the degree of certainty of out-year funding. These problems can be reduced substantially with good up-front planning and a commitment to overcommunication.

### *Official Donors—a Blessing or a Curse?*

Some donors have noted a lack of demand from the private sector for participation in PPPs. For other donors, the demand is substantial and increasing. Some corporations evidence a strong preference to work directly and exclusively with NGOs, whereas others are particularly keen to have an official donor as an active member of the partnership. Understanding these diverse reactions is possible only with a nuanced review of the value propositions and operational constraints of the various parties. This issue has not been studied in any detail, but experience suggests that relatively small details such as the designation of a single access point or portal for PPPs within donor organizations, the establishment of streamlined procedures premised on partnership rather than procurement, and the ability of the donor to invest time and money in discrete transactions do much to improve donors' attractiveness to private sector partners.

### *The Absence of Best Practices in PPP Governance*

Although there is a growing body of experience regarding the governance of PPPs, that experience is not yet well codified or consolidated into a set of best practices, particularly with respect to the role of official donors. Given that many PPPs are established through nonbinding memoranda of understanding or even more informal arrangements, increased attention to issues of governance should be a matter of considerable priority. Among many interesting questions in this regard are the implications of pooled and parallel funding and the markedly different models of how donor agencies choose to participate in the management of alliances they help to fund.

### *Additionality or Corporate Welfare?*

The term "additionality" is frequently used to characterize the *net addition* of resources or results that occurs because of a partnership—in other words, that which would not have happened if the partnership had not occurred.

Typically, each member of a PPP uses the rationale of additionality when presenting projects to its key stakeholders. Corporations usually describe this as "matching" or otherwise extending the funding of their programs. From a public policy perspective, the rationale for investing donor resources in PPPs usually includes the notion that these resources result in net increases in overall funding and development benefits that would not otherwise have occurred. In many cases, both parties claim to have "leveraged" the resources of the other party, even though both parties' expenditures would have occurred with or without the partnership. Though there is little incentive for either party to examine this "additionality premise" critically, stakeholders are becoming increasingly sophisticated in raising this issue.

### *Inside or Outside the Core?*

Some donors argue that—to ensure additionality and minimize any conflict of interest—PPPs should lie outside the core business areas of the corporations involved. At the extreme, this argument favors the use of corporate foundations with an arm's-length relationship to company operations. The creation of CSR units with direct links to corporate front offices is a less extreme version of this model. There is increasing support, however, for the alternative view that scale and sustainability are best ensured when programs lie squarely inside corporations' core business interests. Though there is merit to both views, substantial problems arise when there is even a small measure of confusion or disagreement among the interested parties on this issue.

### *Policies, Transactions, and the Problem of Scale*

Some donors focus their efforts—and their PPPs—on establishing roundtables and oversight mechanisms intended to promote national or global policies, practices, standards, and norms for CSR; labor, environmental, and human rights; or broad-based economic growth. It could be argued that multilateral donors like the United Nations and the World Bank have a comparative advantage with regard to these kinds of initiatives. Other donors focus instead on PPPs that are "projects" in a more traditional sense. These efforts channel donor and private sector funds into transactions intended to deliver concrete benefits to designated target groups in recipient countries. Though these projects often embody or model norms and standards, they do not take as their primary objective the development or dissemination of those norms and standards. A frequently unresolved issue to be addressed in the case of policy interventions is their translation into tangible benefits. An equally important issue to be addressed in the case of transactional programs is achieving scale. Though these issues receive explicit attention in some PPPs, they are more often honored in the breach, leading to disappointed expectations and missed opportunities.

### *Tied Aid*

Some donor countries limit their PPP programs to activities that involve that country's own private sector. While this could be seen as a means for building political support at home or mobilizing a country's private sector as a development partner, it can also be seen as tied aid. In the United States, promotion of the U.S. private sector is a responsibility of the Department of Commerce, the Overseas Private Investment Corporation, the Export-Import Bank, and the Trade and Development Program. For USAID, the only rationale for involving private corporations is to advance development objectives in recipient countries. For that reason, USAID shows no preference for U.S. corporations. This distinction in function does not exist in any other bilateral donor program. Though diversity among donors on this matter poses no obvious difficulty, internal debate regarding this issue in several donor countries runs the risk of undermining support for these programs.

### *PPPs as a Program Area or a Business Model*

Several factors limit the scope of PPPs within donor agencies. Most donors view PPPs almost exclusively in terms of CSR or as a marginal supplement to their other programs for promoting private sector growth. Although most have established units designated to anchor CSR and to serve as points of contact with the private sector, corporate executives express frustration that these units are frequently understaffed and lack access to money and power within their own bureaucracies. Incentives within donor agencies are normally linked to the programming of budgeted funds, not to the leveraging of external resources. Finally, most donors lack mechanisms for incorporating PPPs as part of their strategic planning and country programming when consultations with government and civil society take place and funds are committed. These four factors result in most PPPs being one-off transactions rather than strategic relationships and playing a relatively marginal role in donor programming.

Among the donors reviewed, only USAID has chosen to approach alliance with the private sector as a core business model and to foster the use of this business model across the full range of its development efforts. This has involved staffing and funding a core unit, retraining a large portion of the agency's professional personnel, and changing a variety of operational and procurement procedures. Although some partnerships are also discussed in terms of CSR, USAID's basic rationale for PPPs is leveraging private sector technology and other resources to address the most pressing problems of developing countries; and programs are judged using conventional indicators of development effectiveness. Experience suggests that PPPs are likely to be mainstreamed in other donor agencies only if actively championed by leadership at the highest levels of government and the corporate sector.

### *Failure to Appreciate the Role of Trust and Relationships*

Partnerships are premised on trust—all the more when these partnerships are not legally binding. It is also the case that these agreements often require concurrence at much higher levels than would be required for comparably sized investments of a more conventional sort. Together, these factors constitute a strong argument for beginning with activities that involve leaders at the highest level but that entail modest financial commitments or procedural changes in the first instance. Most official donor agencies are not accustomed to approaching transactions or strategic partnerships in this way.

### *The Emerging Problems of Intellectual Property and Competition*

The decision by some donors to move from a procurement mentality to a partnership model in allocating their funds has implications for how donors regard the intellectual property of their corporate partners and whether they require those partners to "compete" for donor funds. At one extreme, donor funds are seen as a prize, potential partners are treated as sellers, and corporate contributions move into the public domain. At the other extreme, donor funds are seen as an inducement, potential partners are treated as buyers, and corporate contributions remain private property. Donors differ substantially in their positions along this continuum, and few have explicit policies, with obvious implications for the nature of the PPPs in which they participate.

## Conclusion

The discussion above reviews and contrasts recent practices in the use of public-private partnerships between multinational corporations and official donors, and it points to a set of issues that, if not resolved, could undermine this trend or limit its impact. It is clear from this analysis that while misunderstanding remains high and the cultural divide between donors and corporations remains large, the number of success stories is increasing and there is an expanding body of best practices. Among those best practices are the growing recognition that success is most likely when partnerships have strong and evident links to partners' core interests, when partners invest significant time and effort in understanding one another's motives and methods, and when partners retain a clear exit option.

## References

Austin, James E. 2000. *The Collaboration Challenge.* San Francisco: Jossey-Bass.

Grayson, David, and Adrian Hodges. 2004. *Corporate Social Opportunity!* Sheffield, U.K.: Greenleaf Publishing.

Jackson, Ira, and Jane Nelson. 2004. *Profits with Principles: Seven Strategies for Delivering Value with Values.* New York: Random House.

# 9

# *Financing for Global Health*

RAJIV SHAH AND SYLVIA MATHEWS

CURRENT FINANCING FOR GLOBAL HEALTH is not meeting the needs of the developing world. It is critical for private foundations to form partnerships with other nongovernmental organizations and the public and private sectors to help mobilize new resources for global health and to improve the effectiveness of these resources. This short chapter includes a brief overview of development assistance for health (DAH) and a short description of two important public-private initiatives: the Vaccine Fund's International Finance Facility for Immunization (IFFIm) and a description of the World Bank's debt buydowns for successful polio eradication efforts.

## Global Health Challenges

Despite significant advances in global health in the past several decades, citizens of the developing world—particularly children—continue to bear an

**Rajiv Shah** is the director of strategic opportunities at the Bill and Melinda Gates Foundation. He previously served as the foundation's deputy director for policy and finance for global health and as its senior economist. Shah holds a medical degree from the University of Pennsylvania Medical School and a master's of science in health economics from the Wharton School of Business.

**Sylvia Mathews** oversees two of the Bill and Melinda Gates Foundation's grant-making areas: the Global Libraries Program and Strategic Opportunities. A graduate of Harvard University and a Rhodes scholar, she served in the Clinton administration, holding the positions of deputy director of the Office of Management and Budget, deputy chief of staff to the president, and chief of staff to treasury secretary Robert E. Rubin.

unfair burden of disease. Though technologies such as vaccines have led to significant advances in global health, these gains have not been equally shared. Today, one in twelve children dies before the age of five years—mostly from diseases such as respiratory infections, diarrhea, malaria, and measles—and most of these deaths occur in developing countries.

Despite a decline in overall official development assistance in the 1990s, DAH rose in real terms and as a proportion of official development assistance during that time. Since 2000, a series of new funding sources for health, including the Global Fund to Fight AIDS, Tuberculosis, and Malaria, the Vaccine Fund, and special U.S. financing for HIV/AIDS (PEPFAR) have led to further increases in overall spending on health. When including the World Bank's International Development Association (IDA) grants, commitments from all external sources including foundations rose from an annual average of $6.7 billion in 1997–99 to about $9.3 billion in 2002.

Bilateral assistance from donor governments for health rose from $2.2 billion (3.8 percent of the total) to $2.9 billion (6.8 percent) in 2002. (Bilateral expenditures on health do not include contributions to multilateral funds or institutions such as the Global Fund to Fight AIDS, Tuberculosis, and Malaria or the World Bank's International Development Association.) The United States accounted for about 40 percent of the total, even though its share as a percentage of gross domestic product allocated to international development was among the lowest of all the rich countries. The increase in bilateral funding for global health, led by the United States, has continued since 2002, with the introduction of two major new programs, the President's Emergency Plan for HIV/AIDS Relief and the Millennium Challenge Account.

Within the UN system, DAH rose from an annual average of $1.6 billion during the period 1997–99 to $2 billion in 2002. Commitments from the development banks remained stationary at around $1.4 billion—though changes in accounting by the World Bank to include financing for health contained in nonhealth projects (for example, urban, water and sanitation, budget support) suggest that its new commitments for health actually rose from around $1 billion in 2001 to $1.3 billion in 2002 and to $1.7 billion in 2003.

The recent rise in DAH is encouraging but still far short of the volume of external financing for health that has been calculated as "needed" in recent estimates and political pronouncements. On a global level, estimates of what is required from donors to help countries reach the Millennium Development Goals for health have typically been in the range of $15 billion to $35 billion annually. UNAIDS suggested that spending on HIV/AIDS alone in developing countries needed to rise to about $9 billion annually, with around two-thirds of this total to come from external sources. The World Bank calculated a gap of $15 billion to $25 billion in preparation for the Monterrey summit on finance for development. The Commission on Macroeconomics and Health put forward a figure of around $30 billion.

## Effectiveness Is as Important as Additional Funding

More DAH is clearly part of the answer to helping developing countries achieve improved health outcomes and meet the UN Millennium Development Goals. But significant improvements can be made in the effectiveness of health spending. How effective has DAH been, and what can be done to make it more effective?

Development assistance for health has had a mixed record of effectiveness. Despite valid concerns about the overall effectiveness of DAH, there have been large-scale, donor-assisted health programs that have led to significant and sustained improvements in the health of the poor. During the past four decades, donor-funded public health and poverty reduction initiatives have contributed to steady health improvement, as measured by mortality under five years and by life expectancy. Average life expectancy in developing countries was approximately forty in 1950 and is approximately sixty-five today—and most of that improvement has come from a doubling of a child's chances to survive until the age of five. (The onset of the AIDS epidemic in Africa has reversed this trend on that continent.) Even very poor countries with weak institutional environments can effectively implement health improvement programs. For example, tuberculosis control programs and immunization programs in the Democratic Republic of Congo and Myanmar have been successful even during times of civil strife. An analysis completed by the Center for Global Development provides seventeen cases of large-scale health projects, mostly financed by donor assistance, that have led to important improvements in health outcomes that are documented and sustained for more than five years (Levine and others 2004). After reviewing hundreds of programs against criteria including scale, importance, impact, duration, and cost-effectiveness, the center concluded that a wide range of health initiatives have been documented successes. For example, programs to immunize against measles, control river blindness and guinea worm, and fortify salt with iodine all have had a sustained and widespread impact in the developing world. These success stories have generated population health improvements that persist, have achieved success in a broad range of institutional environments, and demonstrate that donor assistance for health can be spent to effectively achieve documented results.

The Center for Global Development analysis, and other reviews of global health activities, indicates that the following factors tend to contribute to positive outcomes:

—strong internal and external political leadership (from donors and governments);

—collaboration across governments, donors, and nongovernmental organizations in program design and implementation;

—consistent, predictable funding support, even after "success" is obtained, from donors and local governments;

—simple and flexible technologies that can be adapted to local conditions;

—programmatic approaches that recognize and address the need to help build health system infrastructure, especially in the area of human resources;

—and household and community participation in the design, execution, and monitoring of program activities.

Other studies support the case examples that indicate that development assistance for health can work, especially in countries with good policy environments. Development assistance to health supports a wide range of activities and services, some focused on specific diseases (polio, tuberculosis, and HIV/AIDS), some on strengthening health systems (disease surveillance, training nurses and midwives), and some on particular services (reproductive and child health services). But development assistance to health does not work as effectively in countries where the policy environment is poor, even though some carefully targeted disease control activities can confer limited benefits in these unfavorable settings. With "good" policies and institutions such as strong property rights, little corruption, and an efficient bureaucracy, an extra 1 percent of gross domestic product in aid is estimated to lead to a decline in infant mortality of 0.9 percent. By contrast, where policies are only average, the decline was only 0.4 percent. And where policies are poor, aid is estimated to have had no significant effect on infant mortality (Burnside and Dollar 1998). Furthermore, development assistance for health can be provided in a manner that undermines efforts to achieve long-term success, regardless of policy environment. Donor funding often is erratic and unpredictable. Short-term time commitments—such as three- to five-year funding windows—prevent recipient countries and programs from planning and investing for the long term and often lead to significant shortages in human resource capacity to implement programs effectively.

Despite such analyses, the overall effectiveness of DAH remains poorly demonstrated and is therefore vulnerable to criticisms that DAH is misspent. A lack of clarity around the overall effectiveness of DAH contributes—in part—to resistance in significantly increasing the resources available to countries with significant health needs. The Bill and Melinda Gates Foundation's work in this sector focuses on expanding resources available to achieve improvements in global health—and enhance the effectiveness of these resources by making financing for global health more long-term, predictable, and results oriented.

## Global Immunization

Vaccination is the most cost-effective way to save a human life, yet limited infrastructure, human resources, and constraints on financing mean children in the developing world continue to die. Nearly 27 million children are not vaccinated in developing countries each year, resulting in nearly 3 million *preventable* deaths a year from diseases like hepatitis B, H. influenza b, measles, tetanus, and pertussis, especially in the poorest parts of the world—Africa and South and Southeast Asia. The largest coverage gaps for vaccination are in parts of Africa and South Asia (with some states in India reported to have vaccine coverage rates of less than 20 percent).

To address this inequity, the Global Alliance for Vaccines and Immunizations (GAVI) funds the introduction of new vaccines and immunization systems' improvement in the seventy-five poorest countries in the world. The alliance raises resources from a range of public and private donors, allows countries to aggregate their purchasing of vaccines from international suppliers, and supports countries in setting and achieving coverage improvements for national immunization programs. The lack of predictable, long-term funding for immunization has been a traditional barrier to improving outcomes. Traditionally, donors provide "just-in-time" funding for countries to purchase vaccines and deliver them to children—and, in fact, many recipient countries will call on a particular donor six to eight weeks before their immunization system has a planned shortage of vaccines and ask for further funding support for an additional vaccine procurement. This system prevents countries from planning and investing in aggressive improvements in immunization coverage and from hiring and training the human resources needed to conduct immunization outreach for hard-to-reach low-income communities. This system also prevents vaccine manufacturers from making large-scale investments (most of which need to be made three to five years before product

**Figure 9-1.** Funds Would Flow to the IFFIm for Use in GAVI's Critical Immunization Efforts

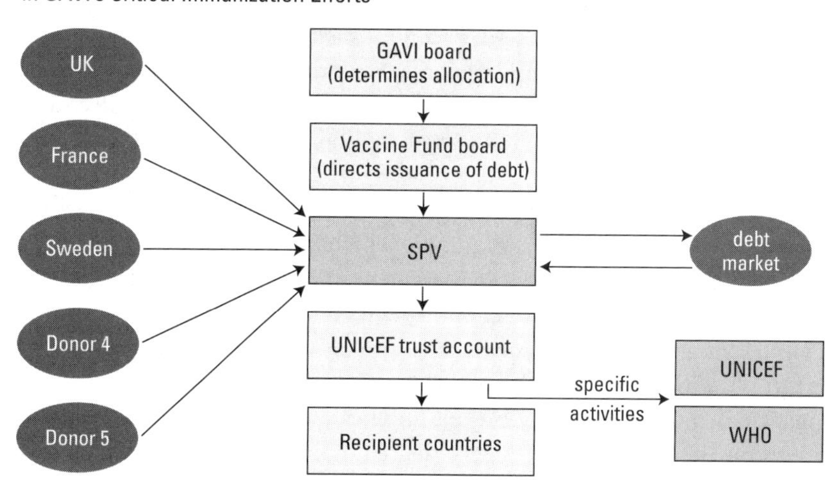


is available) in production facilities capable of producing large volumes of product for the developing world. As a result, high-quality production capacity for vaccines for the developing world has been deteriorating for two decades, resulting in critical shortages, high and unaffordable market prices, and a lack of research and development to create new vaccines specifically for low-income countries.

The GAVI alliance, working with lead funding partners, has developed a $4 billion International Finance Facility for Immunization (IFFIm) to address this problem. The IFFIm will allow GAVI to accept secure, long-term financing commitments (fifteen- to twenty-year commitments) from a variety of donors and to use private capital markets to borrow against those long-term commitments on an as-needed basis to invest in accelerated efforts to support immunization systems in countries or to engage in more effective contracting with vaccine manufacturers (figure 9-1).

This initiative allows countries to plan and pursue expansions of their immunization efforts, manufacturers to pursue new vaccine development and ensure appropriate manufacturing capacity exists to serve poor country markets, and the global public health community to shift from short-term planning to the implementation of a long-term vision of success. Donors will be bound to their commitments as long as certain conditions—which are required for aid effectiveness—are met. (In this case, recipient countries must avoid being in International Monetary Fund arrears to have a continued flow of funds to their immunization programs.) This observable conditionality allows donor governments to score commitments as conditional long-term commitments and allows capital markets to price securities based on these commitments. GAVI will manage the financing arm—and make decisions about when and how to use resources based on effectiveness and long-term financial planning.

The U.K. government has made a specific pledge of $1.8 billion over fifteen years to the IFFIm. In addition, in September 2005 the governments of France, Italy, Norway, and Sweden announced their financial contributions to the IFFIm (bringing total commitments to $4 billion), and now other countries are considering participating in this innovative new financing effort. The program would provide long-term, predictable, and flexible financing, and GAVI already is exploring new ways to allow recipient countries to make longer-term, results-oriented investments in their immunization systems and to contract with manufacturers to develop and manufacture new vaccines that would help save lives in the developing world. The World Health Organization estimates that a $4 billion IFFIm would save more than 5 million lives in the next decade (GAVI 2004). It also would serve as a model demonstrating how secure long-term financial commitments can improve the effectiveness of global immunization programming (figure 9-2).

## Debt Buydowns to Support Polio Eradication

Poliomyelitis (polio) is a highly infectious disease caused by a virus that invades the nervous system and can cause total paralysis in a matter of hours and death—usually from an inability to breathe. Although there is no cure, an effective polio vaccine and an aggressive public health campaign to eradicate the disease have led to an elimination of the disease in wealthy nations and a reduction in the number of developing world cases from 350,000 in 1988 to just under 700 cases reported at the end of 2003. Nearly all of these remaining cases are in specific parts of Asia and Africa.

The last steps of disease elimination and eradication are typically geographically localized, concentrated on a small number of cases, and costly. Elimination occurs when no new reported cases (in contexts with strong monitoring capacity) exist. The World Health Organization declares a disease as eradicated in a certain region after elimination and several other conditions (no cases appear for a certain number of years) have been met. As a result, countries pursuing disease eradication do so when the prevalence and

**Figure 9-2.** IFFIm Would Add $2 Billion to $4 Billion in Expected Traditional Fundraising, Allowing for a Unique Disbursement Profile that Maximizes Lives Saved—5 Million through 2015

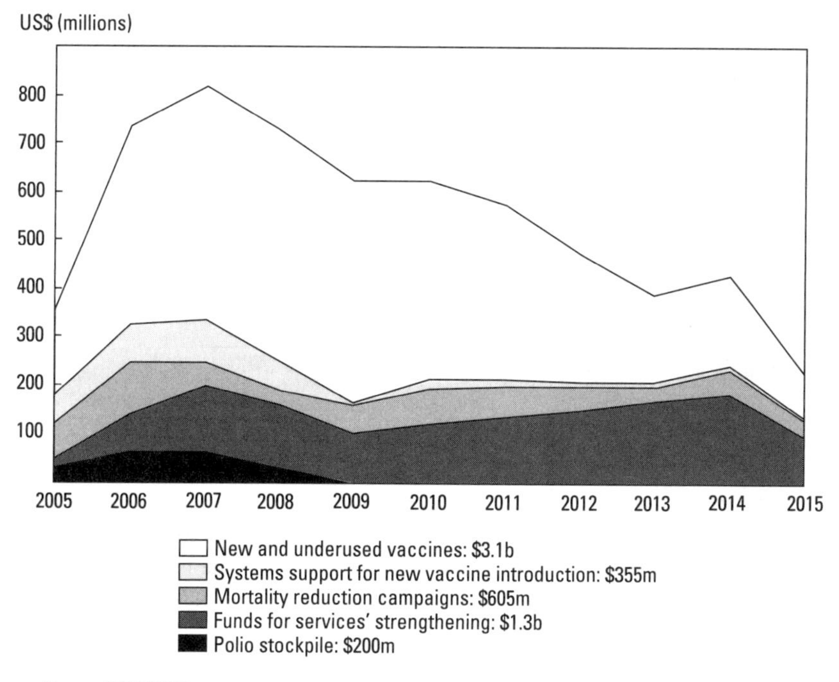


Source: GAVI (2004).

burden of the disease are small relative to other preventable causes of mortality or morbidity—resulting in countries incurring large costs of eradication but with far fewer direct health benefits. In fact, most of the benefits of eradication accrue to the global community (and therefore disease eradication constitutes an important global public good). As a result, an appropriate and effective financing tool would allow donor countries to cover the costs of the final stages of global disease eradication.

The Bill and Melinda Gates Foundation has collaborated with the World Bank, Rotary International, and the UN Foundation to respond to this need by establishing a trust fund to buy down the principal and interest on World Bank IDA loans taken by countries to pursue the final stages of polio eradication. Once a country takes an IDA loan to pursue polio eradication efforts, the World Health Organization's Polio Eradication Initiative assists the country in carrying out eradication tasks (including establishing an appropriate

**Figure 9-3.** Bill and Melinda Gates Foundation–World Bank–Rotary International–UN Foundation Partnership Creates Incentives for Polio Eradication Efforts in High-Risk Countries

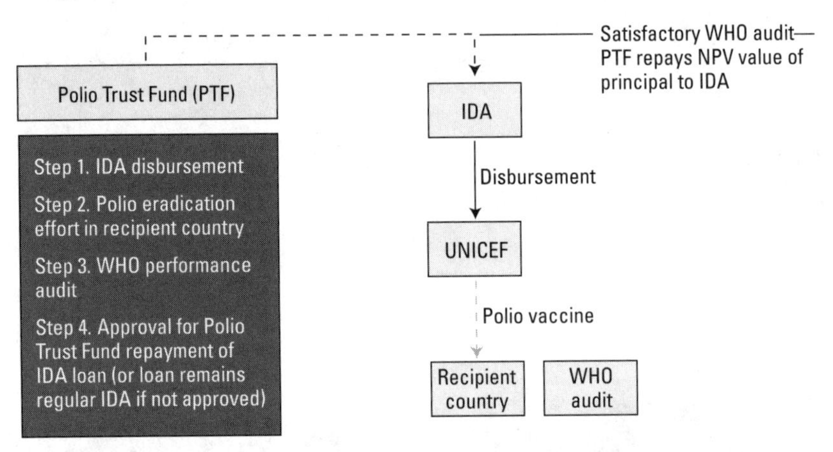


monitoring system) and in certifying successful completion of the elimination and eradication program. Once certification is achieved, the trust fund repays the World Bank for the outstanding balance on the loan on behalf of the recipient country. Nigeria and Pakistan already have used this funding mechanism, and India and other IDA countries in Africa are working to use this mechanism as well (figure 9-3).

This financing arrangement provides important benefits to most involved parties. Countries receive subsidized loans to initiate eradication program activities with the promise that if they successfully complete the WHO's program the payments on the loan will be covered by donors. In that manner, the subsidized nature of IDA lending and the resources from the trust fund provide additional financing to countries pursuing polio eradication. Donors are able to leverage their funding (buying down already subsidized loans) to achieve a specific outcome and only spend funds once results have been achieved. The World Bank has been able to rapidly fund the implementation of a turnkey program—the Polio Eradication Initiative—with a focus on improved effectiveness. The buydown structure creates incentives for effective program implementation by rewarding good performance and using a credible performance audit as a trigger for taking on the obligations of a project loan. The World Bank estimates that through this results-oriented program more than 65 million polio immunizations have been provided, and it awarded this program its Presidential Excellence Award.

## Conclusion

Systematic reviews of the case examples have demonstrated that development assistance for health can be provided in a manner that is highly effective at achieving sustained improvements in global health. However, despite current increases in DAH, little is known about the overall effectiveness of this health spending. Examples such as the International Finance Facility for Immunization and the polio buydowns are new efforts to demonstrate that focused, results-oriented funding that is flexible but also highly predictable over longer time frames can be highly effective at saving lives throughout the developing world.

## References

Burnside, Craig, and Dollar, David. 1998. "Aid, the Incentive Regime, and Poverty Reduction." Policy Research Working Paper 1937. June. Washington, D.C.: World Bank.

Global Alliance for Vaccines and Immunization (GAVI). 2004. "A Proposal for an International Finance Facility for Immunization (IFFIm)." October 6.

Levine, Ruth, and others. 2004. *Millions Saved: Proven Successes in Global Health.* Washington, D.C.: Brookings, Global Economy and Development Center.

# *Index*

## THE BROOKINGS INSTITUTION

The Brookings Institution is a private nonprofit organization devoted to research, education, and publication on important issues of domestic and foreign policy. Its principal purpose is to bring the highest quality independent research and analysis to bear on current and emerging policy problems. The Institution was founded on December 8, 1927, to merge the activities of the Institute for Government Research, founded in 1916, the Institute of Economics, founded in 1922, and the Robert Brookings Graduate School of Economics and Government, founded in 1924. Interpretations or conclusions in Brookings publications should be understood to be solely those of the authors.